THE PATRIOT TEST

Americans Grading George W. Bush and John Kerry

THE PATRIOT TEST

★ ★ ★ ★ ★ ★ ★ ★ ★ ★ ★ ★ ★ ★ ★

Americans Grading George W. Bush and John Kerry

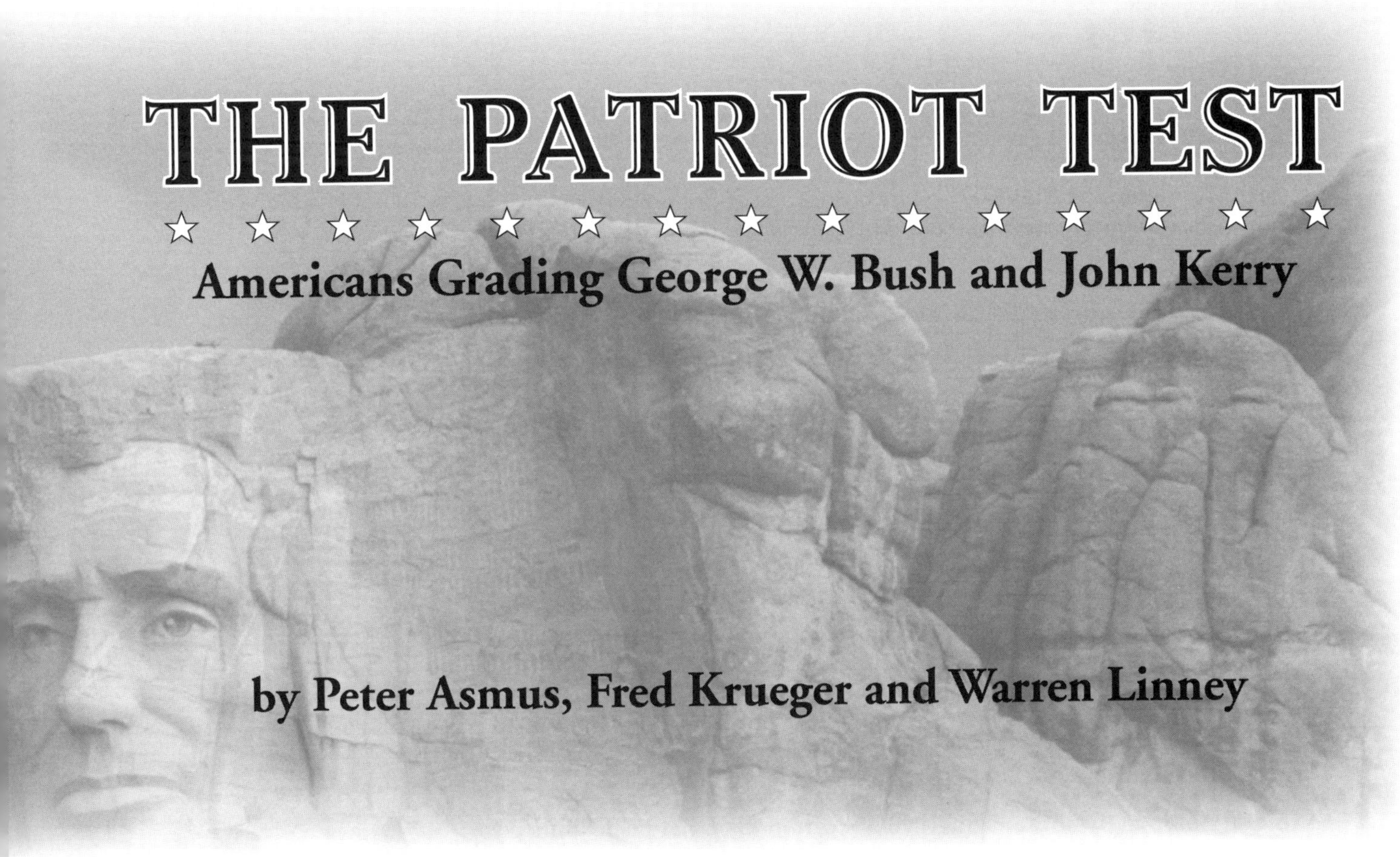

by Peter Asmus, Fred Krueger and Warren Linney

Published by Patriotic Press, LLC

www.patrioticpress.org

(800) 732-0860

For information on bulk sales please contact us at bulksales@patriottest.org.
For information on book tours or educational use go to the website at www.patriottest.org

Cover and book design by Gabriel Graubner, The Electronic Monastery, elecmon@sonic.net

Typography: Adobe Garamond, ITC Cheltenham Handtooled, Carta

Cover stock: 10 pt CIS; text paper: 60# White Offset Vellum

Cover photograph of Mount Rushmore by Andrea Komoczi; John Kerry photo by Sharon Farmer; George W. Bush, UN/DPI Photo; Jobs and Economy, USDA photo; Homeland Security photograph by James R. Tourtellate; Foreign Policy, UN/DPI Photo by Eskinder Debebe; Education, Family Values, and Environment photographs by Gabriel Graubner

ISBN 0-9759387-0-3

First printing August 2004 in the United States of America

Library of Congress Cataloging-in-Publication Data has been applied for

ACKNOWLEDGEMENTS

We would like to thank all the people who contributed to this labor of love for our country. This book was a group effort of brainstorming and positive critique of each other's ideas. It reminded us of the Constitutional Convention in its passion, focus and length. Through all the incredible work, we knew it was vitally important to help voters decide on the candidate with the best patriotic policies and actions.

We want to especially thank Bruce E. Kennedy for his writing and help in keeping this book on track in many ways. Pamela Hall was like Lady Liberty, keeping the torch lit for the project. All the associate editors were invaluable for their research and editing skills: Pamela Conley, Tony Seton, Gretchen Amer, Kati Broomhead, Aaron Chan, Maximus, Gwyn Kirk, Larry McCowan, Michael Brew, Linda Sartor, and Eileen Hegel. We appreciate Vincent Rossi, for his contribution to the introduction and Brian Narelle for assisting with the content and title of the book.

Tim McAllister helped the book move forward and establish its distribution.

Gabriel Graubner from the Electronic Monastery did more than just design the cover and layout: he was the final glue that put the book together.

Finally, thanks to our spouses, children, parents and friends who gave us inspiration and encouragement and were understanding of the amount of time we spent trying to do our small part in making this country better.

TABLE OF CONTENTS

PATRIOTISM, PIETY AND POLITICS

> *"In my inaugural address, I asked Americans to seek a common good beyond their comfort; to serve their nation, beginning with their neighbor."*
> ~ George W. Bush, On God and Country, p. 189.

> *"Patriotism is the courage to fight for those things that strengthen and defend our nation."*
> ~ Senator John Kerry, April 14, 2002.

A patriot is defined as "a person who loves his country and zealously defends its interests." Patriotism describes the actions of anyone who works selflessly for the best interests of their country and its citizens.

Recent polls show that 90% of Americans consider themselves to be patriotic or proud to be an American. How can these patriots decide which presidential candidate will act in the best interests of our country?

The Patriot Test is designed to help you choose which of the two leading candidates will best uphold the founding principles of America. Included in this book, are the words and actions of President George W. Bush and Senator John Kerry. You will be able to put the candidates through *The Patriot Test* and compare their records to the founding principles and give them a grade.

The separation of church and state is unquestionably one of the philosophical bedrocks of American political life. But does this fact mean that piety (reverence toward God) and patriotism (love of country) are never supposed to mix? The truth is that piety and patriotism are two streams that flow from a single deep well of human feeling.

"God Bless America," sometimes called "America's unofficial national anthem," is a perfect example. It is essentially a prayer set to music. We are asking God to bless America, to "stand beside her and guide her through the night with the light from above." But why do we ask God to bless America? Because, as the song says, this is "the land that I love," my "home sweet home." In short, the song is a reflection of the fact that fervent patriotic feeling often compels patriots to pray for our country.

Another example of the marriage of piety and patriotism may be found at Arlington National Cemetery. The sign that greets the visitor says, "Welcome to Arlington National Cemetery, Our Nation's Most Sacred Shrine, Please Remember, These Are Hallowed Grounds." The words "sacred" and "hallowed" are religiously weighted words, yet they are associated with the greatest act of patriotism possible, dying for one's country.

If the ultimate act of patriotism is to give your life for your country, the ultimate act of love, according to the Gospel of John (15:13), is to lay down one's life for one's friends. The ultimate act of piety is to sacrifice one's life for the love of God. There is a link between our families, our friends, our country and our faith in God. The "civic" sacredness evoked by patriotic sacrifice parallels the "spiritual" sacredness of religious sacrifice.

America has traditionally commanded respect around the world because of fundamentally new concepts of freedom of speech and freedom of religion that have changed the way people view government's roles in their lives. But what exactly are our patriotic principles? And how do we distinguish between our duties as patriots in the political process and our obligations to our Christian faith?

Foundations of our Country

Understanding the early history of this nation sheds some important light on the unique relationship between faith in God and our political processes here in the U.S. Our patriotic principles were shaped by the words and actions of the first settlers who came to the New World.

It was the Puritans escaping from England who articulated radical new notions about government and God. Self-sacrifice and frugality were balanced with the notion that self-interest should not succumb to vice. Based on these ideals, the Puritans set out to construct an unprecedented republic in the New World.

Believing that the Church of England had become corrupt, their solution was to come to the New World and worship as they pleased. They became known as "free thinkers" since they argued that a King, the Catholic Pope, or other forms of aristocracy, did not have to play any intermediate role in religious worship. According to the Puritans, each individual had a direct link to God. In 1623, John Winthrop built a colony in Massachusetts based on what he called a Covenant. He believed that he and his fellow Puritans were chosen on a special mission from God to come to America. There, all members of the colony would live according to the precepts of Christian charity.

Then, in 1774, John Locke declared a fundamental truth: "a universal law governs the Universe through the acquisition of knowledge acquired by reason." According to Locke, human beings created governments and human beings therefore could alter them. That same year, Thomas Paine wrote "Common Sense," a book that sold 120,000 copies in only three months. This book advocated a republican form of government totally distinct from England. It also allowed greater representation. Why should the right to vote be limited to the elite and landowners when all people could directly access the divine? It was this combination of belief in God, and an open political process, that set the stage for our Founding Fathers to declare independence.

Patriotic Principles

Today, our patriotic principles are the values that students typically learn in U.S. history classes in school. The principles are noted below in bold type. Perhaps these words penned by Thomas Jefferson at the beginning of Declaration of Independence sum it up best:

> *We hold these truths to be self-evident, that* ***all men are created equal****, that they are endowed by their Creator with certain inalienable Rights, that among these are* ***Life, Liberty and the pursuit of Happiness****. That to secure these Rights, Governments are instituted among Men, deriving their just powers from the consent of the governed....*

These principles invigorated the colonies. Influenced by Winthrop, Locke and Paine, these values were articulated as universal truths by Founding Fathers like Thomas Jefferson as he drafted the document that declared our separation from England. As the signers of that Declaration of Independence enunciated these values, they announced to the world their intent to establish a new country built upon a set of inalienable rights of the people.

The principles of patriotism are contained in documents written long ago which still shape our ideals and identity as a country. Along with the Declaration of Independence, they include the *Preamble to the Constitution*, *The Bill of Rights*, and the inspiring addresses of our great presidents.

In the book *Our Sacred Honor*, William Bennett writes: "Americans are rightfully proud to possess the world's longest lasting and most imitated written political document — the Constitution." Revisit the fifty-two words contained in the Preamble to the Constitution and feel the strength of its ideals.

We the People of the United States, in Order to ***form a more perfect Union, establish Justice, ensure domestic Tranquility, provide for the common Defense, promote the general Welfare, and secure the Blessing of Liberty to ourselves and our Posterity,*** *do ordain and establish this Constitution for the United States of America.*

"We the People," refers to the fact that the people approved the Constitution through state conventions, not by state legislatures. Chief Justice John Marshall wrote "the government proceeds directly from the people." Government is "ordained and established in the name of the people.... Its powers are granted by them and are to be exercised correctly on them and for their benefit."

Contemporary Patriotism's Link To The Past

The people that personify our patriotic principles – Washington, Jefferson, Madison, and Adams – acted with great sacrifice. Washington once wrote, "When my country demands sacrifice, personal ease must always be a secondary consideration." They shunned personal gain to create a new form of government that was "for the people, by the people and of the people."

Many of the 56 men who signed the Declaration of Independence suffered immensely because of their staunch belief in freedom and the great promise of a United States of America. A mix of lawyers, merchants and farmers, these educated citizens knew their signatures on the Declaration of Independence could carry a heavy price. Five were captured and tortured by the British before they died. Twelve of them had their homes ransacked and burned; nine died from wounds or afflictions resulting from the Revolutionary War.

The patriots who established a republican form of government in America not only risked their lives. They gambled on human nature. They trusted in America's spiritual fortitude. As George Washington said in his first inaugural address in 1789: "The preservation of the sacred fire of liberty and the destiny of the republican model of government are justly considered…deeply…finally, staked on the experiment entrusted to the hands of the American people." Through it all, Washington and his fellow patriots kept their vision of creating a new nation dedicated to a self-evident truth that all people are created equal and free.

A rich patriotic tradition has continued throughout the decades. Here are the words of some modern patriots about the high standards this nation aspires to reach:

Duty, honor, country. Those three hallowed words reverently dictate what you ought to be, what you can be, what you will be. They are your rallying point to build courage when courage seems to fail, to regain faith when there seems to be little cause for faith, to create hope when hope becomes forlorn. ~ General Douglas MacArthur

Of all the nations of today, the future will say that there were two kinds: those that were intelligent, courageous, decisive and tireless in their support of high principle – and those that disappeared from the earth. The true patriots of today are those who are giving their best to assure that our own country will always be found in the first of these two categories ~ President Dwight David Eisenhower

With a good conscience our only sure reward, with history as the final judge of our deeds, let us go forth to lead the land we love, asking His blessing and His help, but knowing that here on earth, God's work must truly be our own. ~ President John F. Kennedy

Here is the fabric of America. Ever since the founding of the Republic, citizens have bonded to these cherished principles: **freedom of speech and religion; due process and equal protection under the law; universal access to education; economic security**; and, an ability, through hard work and ingenuity, to **seek a better life**. These ideals gave Lincoln the right to claim that America might yet be the "last best hope" for people everywhere. They inspired Justice Hugo Black to declare that America's patriotic idealism was "a Constitutional faith." We have faith that our government will function according to these principles and to the articles in the Constitution that specify a **separation of powers, institutional checks and balances, and free and fair elections**. The question for you to decide is whether or not these principles are being followed by the actions of our presidential candidates.

Dimensions of patriotism have been examined for centuries. Patriotism to some means "My country right or wrong," as Stephen Decatur declared. To others, patriotism is opposition to tyranny, and the right to dissent. Theodore Roosevelt gave us this pointed lesson about patriotism in 1918: "To announce that there must be no criticism of the president, or that we are to stand by the president, right or wrong, is not only unpatriotic and servile, but is morally treasonable to the American public."

Patriotism can be a paradox. We can try to resolve these seeming inconsistencies by testing whether government policies – whether proposed or already adopted – seem to serve and further the founding principles of this nation. If we apply *The Patriot Test* as we judge the presidential candidates, we'll rarely be faced with a dilemma of "my country, right or wrong."

Republican Abraham Lincoln, one of our greatest presidents, also declared "that this nation, under God, shall have a new birth of freedom, and that government of the people, by the people and for the people shall not perish from the earth." An essential requirement of our citizen-based democracy is that it can only work if its members participate to keep it healthy and functioning.

Citizen participation is not only a patriotic duty and a commitment to making this country a better place. It is a responsibility to be well informed and to be active in the democratic process.

Faith and the Political Process

The Patriot Test also helps the reader discern how today's candidates for president follow Christian teachings in carrying out their duties. Like the documents that founded this country, the Scriptures have shaped the political subconscious of America. Regardless of how one has understood the Bible, its principles have fortified the way America understands patriotism.

While the religious practices of the Founding Fathers differed, they were united in respect for the Bible as fundamental to Christian and Jewish faith. Most of the Founding Fathers grew up in a religious atmosphere. They believed that spiritual freedom was a foundation and bulwark for political freedom. With that freedom under law we would govern ourselves.

Our Founding Fathers understood that religious belief carried moral and social implications. Because it was entirely appropriate for people to express these beliefs through their political activities, the links between Christianity and American patriotism still run deep. The motto "In God We Trust" is therefore proclaimed on our coins. Every newly elected president takes a solemn oath of office with his hand placed upon a Bible. References to God sprinkle the writings of the original patriots who set the stage for the American system of government.

Of course, great philosophers of the Old World also considered both patriotism and piety to be virtues. For Plato and Aristotle, these concepts were the necessary foundations of all human life. Morality hinged upon four "cardinal" virtues: wisdom (or prudence), justice, fortitude and temperance. In *"The Republic,"* Plato builds his system of virtues upon the analogy of the state (or government) with the human soul. These four most fundamental principles of the conduct of human life appear in the structure of society because they are fundamental in the structure of the soul.

These four cardinal virtues are also praised in the Scriptures under other names in many places. The classic lists of virtues in the Scriptures are the following: Isaiah 11:2-5 *(the seven gifts of the Spirit)*; Matthew 5:3-12 and Luke 6:20-26 *(the beatitudes)*; 1 Corinthians 13:4-7 *(the hymn to love)*; Galatians 5:22 *(the fruit of the Spirit)*; 2 Peter 1:5-7 *(the virtues)*. Some other important New Testament passages on virtues are: Romans 5:1-5; I Timothy 6:11; Ephesians 4:1-3, 32; 2 Timothy 2:22-25; Colossians 3:12-15; Titus 2:1-5, 12; Philippians 4:8; Titus 3:1-2.

Underlying these virtues is the Judeo-Christian concept of the human being as the image of God. Humans are responsible for aligning their actions with these virtues in accordance with the will and the design of the Creator. This responsibility to God is the basis of the inalienability of all human rights. All human rights – from whatever source – are the object of justice. The purpose of government is to protect all rights of citizens for the common good. Authority is given to the state or government, as Scripture teaches, by God. Such is the timeless, perennial teaching of the Judeo-Christian religious tradition and most of Western Civilization.

We see therefore from history, from the heritage of our Western philosophical tradition, and from Scripture itself, that patriotism and piety both spring from the same fountainhead in the human heart. Patriotism and piety belong together as virtues under the principal virtue of justice. Therefore, it is unjust to criticize or condemn any political leader simply because he or she seems to link patriotism and piety in their political activities.

At the same time, to preach piety and patriotism in the political arena carries with it the obligation to realize, as far as is humanly possible, true justice for all. History will—and the electorate should—judge a political leader on the conduct of his or her office, not on his or her personal religious faith. But if a leader says that his religious faith is important for him in the conduct of his office, it is then incumbent upon the electorate to examine his or her actions in light of his or her faith in order to see if that statement is a meaningful reflection of character and competence.

Let The Test Begin

This book eliminates the distorting rhetoric of modern media-based political campaigns and returns to the Founding Principles in order for Americans to better understand the current choices. *The Patriot Test* compares the words of the candidates and their current campaign spin to their actual records throughout their political careers. It is an interactive book that allows readers to decide for themselves which candidate's policies and actions are the most patriotic.

An informed electorate is key to making democracy work. You may be surprised what you discover, or you may feel validated by your current views. Either way, *The Patriot Test* will help you uncover and perhaps rediscover what makes America great.

You, the reader, will grade how well Bush and Kerry have lived up to the principles of patriotism as defined by our Founding Fathers and other patriots over the past two and a half centuries. In order to be concise, we use the word "patriotic" in most of the test questions. You may want to substitute the phrase "how much in the best interests of our country" for the word "patriotic" to help you grade the candidates.

With this book in your hand, you will no longer be passively watching this exciting campaign unfold, but will be an active part of this race for America's future. You can use the information in this book to write a letter to your local newspaper or church bulletin, and discuss these issues with your neighbors. Using the enclosed bookmark, you will enter the candidates' scores based on a 5 point rating scale similar to grades ranging from A to F that are given in school.

Remember that what is right for this country will also be right for its citizens. Let us then, with diligence and care, seek out the records of the candidates that we might vote, not merely for a party or for a position on one issue, but for the high road of patriotism. In this way, we will not only choose rightly for our country, but we will place a spotlight on the actions of our political leaders that will only grow brighter in the years ahead.

The message of this book is one of hope. We realize that there are currently many challenges facing the United States. By choosing a president that upholds the patriotic principles that created our nation, each of us can help realize the goals of the founding fathers for which America still stands.

"Independence Forever" ~ spoken by James Madison while
proposing a toast to celebrate America's 50th anniversary

Independence Forever,
Peter Asmus, Fred Krueger and Warren Linney
July 4, 2004

This book is dedicated to all the original men and women patriots who created a new concept of government and struggled to fulfill their dreams; to all the patriots since Independence that kept the fires of freedom and equality burning bright for the world to see; and, to our citizens who now work to make this country better for us and for future generations.

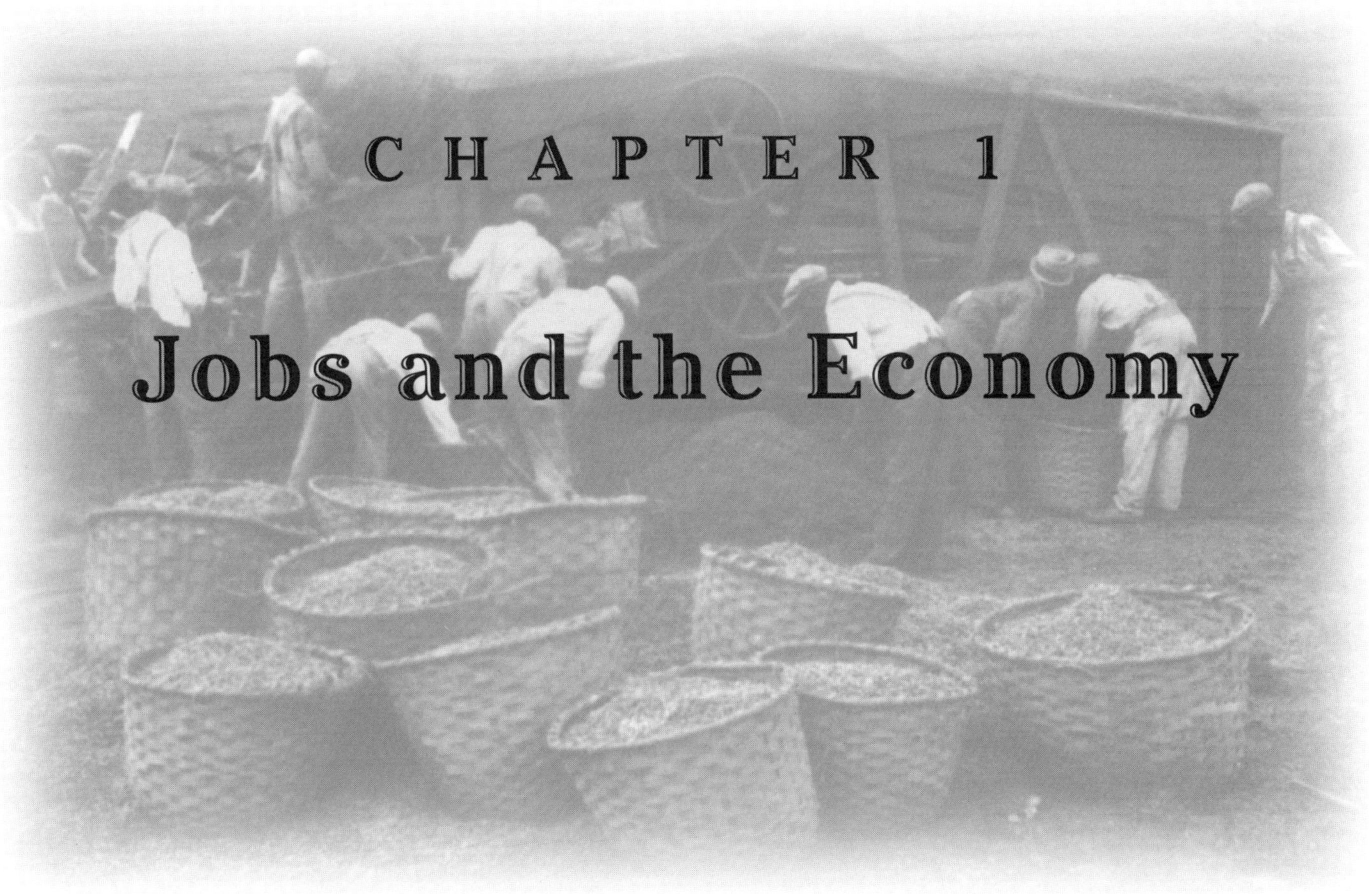

CHAPTER 1

Jobs and the Economy

INTRODUCTION

Look up the word "economy" in the dictionary and you may be surprised at what you find. While many of us fret about the economy today – and perhaps lament the go-go years of the recent past – few of us have probably paused to think about what "the economy" actually is. We tend to project that it is something "out there" and separate from us, when, in reality, we are all part of it.

Here are some dictionary definitions of economy:

- *The management of income and expenditures of a household, private business, community or government;*
- *A careful management of wealth or resources; avoidance of waste by careful planning and use; thrift or thrifty use;*
- *Restrained or efficient use of one's materials or technique;*
- *A system of producing, distributing and consuming wealth.*

It is this last meaning that perhaps best fits the context of this discussion, though the word "economy" obviously implies careful efficient management characterized by thrifty restraint. Systems of economy create the jobs that distribute the wealth throughout society. The economy is therefore a fundamental building block of modern civilization.

It was also an important bedrock for the Biblical community. In the Bible, Christians read speeches by patriarchs, prophets and Jesus, himself, that relate to economic life.

> *"Can a Christian imagine Jesus walking through Galilee, urging everyone to pursue his or her own selfish interests, to seek personal financial gain and not worry about the needs of others? Would it not be nearer the spirit of Christ to say that everyone should lovingly pursue the well-being of each member of the human family, thus cooperating with God in assuring the common good? The only invisible hand in Christian teaching is the hand of God, and when we grasp it, we are led away from self-interest to love our neighbor as ourselves."*[1]

Jesus possessed a profound sense of economic justice, and he calls Christians to account for it in their lives.

America has always had a peculiar relationship with the notion of economy. In response to the aristocracies and traditional European ways of managing economic activities, Americans possessed an almost divine belief in the power of money to distribute itself where it was best needed. Hence, Adam Smith's "invisible

[1] Richard K. Taylor, *Economics and the Gospel* (Philadelphia: United Church Press, 1973), pg. 12

hand" behind a free market was an optimistic idea that captured the imagination of a very young America. Yet these patriots also believed that their new government had an obligation to provide for a basic safety net of social services for all citizens.

After all, this was a government for and by the people. The Preamble of the Constitution declares that "promoting the general welfare" of Americans is one of the critical functions of the new democratic republican government. Another lofty ideal contained in this Preamble is the goal to "form a more perfect union." Like Scriptures, many things can be read into the meaning of this phrase. In a perfect world, all Americans would have adequate resources to pursue life, liberty and the pursuit of happiness.

Remember, what made America unique in the eyes of the world was that it represented equal opportunity for all. Consider this observation of Marquis de Lafayette in 1777:

> *What charms me is, that all citizens are brethren. In America, there are no poor, nor even what we call peasantry. Each individual has his own honest property, and the same rights as the wealthiest landowner.*

Many of the Founding Fathers foresaw a small government. This was a reasonable reaction against the governance systems of Europe, which more often than not served the very rich and few instead of the poor and many. There were great disparities that had been reinforced by governing institutions that were shaped by feudal systems in which the majority of people owned no land and had very little opportunity to achieve independent financial success.

America was a breath of fresh air. That's why it became a magnet for so many people seeking to live "the American dream" – owning one's home. Yes, private property, and being free to make and sell whatever one wanted in a free and open economy were radical steps indeed. And America's abundant resources provided the perfect playground for a variety of capitalists to start up their own businesses and get a healthy piece of the proverbial economic pie.

Of course, as the nation grew, and times changed, so did the challenges facing federal as well as state and local governments. The complexity of civilization rendered concepts such as "free market" and even "liberty" as ideals tempered somewhat by time. Particularly challenging was the 20th century. Two world wars and the Great Depression were cataclysmic events that inspired great shifts in the role government played in our lives. Perhaps one of the best examples of how increasing levels of government intervention became justified was the advent of electricity.

It was the advent of huge monopolies that served the lifeblood of modern society – electricity – that greatly expanded the scope of government regulation in our lives. It was Democratic President Franklin D. Roosevelt that created the modern welfare state with his New Deal. A key economic development aspect of the New Deal created government agencies that would deliver cheap hydroelectricity to parts of rural America that private utilities refused to serve. The idea of Social Security also gained popular support during this time period in light of the instability Americans witnessed between the Great Depression and the end of World War II.

The New Deal programs started losing their luster in the '80s with the election of Republican Ronald Reagan. The tax code was simplified and the so-called "welfare state" began to shrink. The scale of government had grown in sheer size and specialization that would have surely shocked our Founding Fathers. Surprisingly enough, it was the United Kingdom that joined the U.S. in its efforts to shift greater portions of the economy from the public to the private sectors. This trend continues today. Globalization and other recent developments in economic activity offer new opportunities to experiment with the words and wisdom of our Founding Fathers to see how that wisdom might apply to the economic challenges facing the U.S. today.

Median Income

"From everyone who has been given much, much will be required." Luke 12:48

> ***"The Bush tax cuts benefit all Americans, but reserve the greatest percentage reduction for the lowest income families."***
> **~ George W. Bush: A Tax Cut With a Purpose December 1, 1999**

> ***"Under this Administration, America's middle class has been abandoned – its dreams denied, its Main Street interests ignored and its mainstream values scorned by a White House that puts privilege first."***
> **~ John Kerry, www.johnkerry.com/issues/economy**

Promoting the general welfare of Americans has always been a top priority of our Presidents down through the ages. Though the issues each faced over the past 200 years have always been different, the goal of the nation's economic programs generally professed to be egalitarian in nature. In other words, they were designed to lift all citizens up in their pursuit of the good life.

America has always set up very high ideals for itself. And included among these high ideals was the idea that all Americans could share the wealth. This was the land of opportunity, a land where everyone could pursue "the American Dream," by owning one's own house, and live comfortably regardless of one's social status, ethnic background, or gender.

One of the key statistics used to determine how well any President's economic plan is working is "median income," a measure that captures the income level at which an even number of Americans make more and an even number make less. The median income is assumed to be the better indicator of the health of the economy since it more accurately depicts the income level actually enjoyed by the most Americans. In 2002, the inflation adjusted median income in 2002 was $42,409, a drop of 3.3% compared to 2000, the year President Bush was elected.[2]

[2] Peter G. Gosselin, "US Incomes Falling, Poverty Rate Rising," *Los Angeles Times*, September 27, 2003.

As with all statistics, one still has to be careful in drawing conclusions. There are so many factors that can influence the median income figures. For example, the large influx of immigrants into the U.S. has lowered the nation's median income, as has the growing number of teenagers entering the work force and working for low wages.[3]

Still, the Federal Reserve and other sources have recently reported that the difference in median net wealth (a measure that includes other sources of wealth beyond just income) between the 10% of the families with the highest incomes and the 20% of families with the lowest income jumped 70% from 1998 through 2001. The median net worth gap between whites and minorities grew by 21% during the same time period.[4]

The richest 1% of Americans holds more than 38% of the nation's wealth, a concentration of wealth unmatched in any developed country.[5]

Q: Should improving the median income of all Americans be a top priority of the U.S. President?

President Bush's Record

The focus of President George W. Bush's economy recovery plan has been tax cuts enacted first in 2001 and then a subsequent tax cut package – The President's Jobs and Growth Act of 2003 – passed in 2003. While most of these tax cuts were targeted at individual taxpayers, the Bush Administration has also successfully pushed through dividend and capital gains tax relief. Elements of the Bush Administration programs aimed at middle-class families also included the following: reduction in the so-called

Senator Kerry's Record

Senator Kerry has claimed that his first economic priority is to replace the 3 million jobs that have been lost since President Bush took office (roughly a third of these jobs were already restored in early 2004). His long-term goal is to create 10 million jobs in his first four years in office, an ambitious goal, but one which falls far short of the achievements of the Clinton Administration, which added almost 23 million jobs over two-terms, the most jobs added to the economy in U.S. history.[6]

---

[3] Dr. Sherry Cooper, "Things Proved Better Than Portrayed," BMO Nesbitt Burns Economic Research, May 2004.

[4] Barbara Hagenbaugh, "Nation's Wealth Disparity Widens," *USA Today*, January 22, 2003.

[5] Peter Singer, *The President of Good and Evil: The Ethics of George W. Bush*, Dutton Books: The Penguin Group, New York, NY.

[6] Federal Bureau of Labor Statistics: www.bls.gov.

Bush's Record

"marriage penalty;" a faster increase in the child tax credit; an immediate implementation of a new and lower 10% tax bracket. According to Bush Administration figures, the average tax rebate for 91 million U.S. taxpayers in 2003 was $1,126.[7]

Despite the Bush Administration's efforts in the economy, the federal Census Bureau has reported that median household income fell 1.1% in 2002. During the first two years that President Bush was in office, median household income fell by $1,419. African Americans and Hispanics experienced the most significant declines. The lingering recession in the U.S. also has taken its toll on the poor. The federal Census Bureau also reports that poverty rose up to 12.1% of the population in 2002, up from 11.7% in 2001. That translates into 1.7 million new citizens becoming classified as living in poverty. The number of poor people in the U.S. has grown to 34.6 million, of which almost a third are children. The poverty level stood at 11.3% in 2000.

The poverty rate had declined consistently throughout the 1990s.[8] Today, the U.S. is the only country among the 19 wealthiest nations to feature a double-digit poverty rate.[9] The Labor Department reported in early June that jobs increased for three consecutive months between

Kerry's Record

Kerry is considered one of the "New Democrats," members of the Democratic Party who are more supportive of business interests and pushing new technologies into the mainstream than some of their counterparts. Among Kerry's primary changes to current policy in Washington, DC is to rollback the tax cuts President Bush has put into place for the wealthiest Americans. But he has proposed to keep the tax cuts for middle class and lower-income Americans in place.

Unlike Bush, Kerry supports an increase in the minimum wage. His campaign has pointed out that the current minimum wage is 19% below the 1979 level in inflation-adjusted terms.[10] This represents a 30-year low in terms of the real purchasing power of the minimum wage. The minimum wage would have to be raised to $8.14 for workers to have the same purchasing power they had in 1969. Senator Kerry helped lead the fight to pass the last increase in the minimum wage increase in 1997.

Kerry has received a 90% voting record from the AFL-CIO over his 18-year Senate career, but has consistently flunked scorecards published by Americans For Tax Reform and National Taxpayers Union Foundation. Yet when Lieutenant Governor of Massachusetts, Kerry also supported much of the Reagan Administration's shift

[7] *The President's Economic Security Agenda:* http://georgewbush.com/Economy/Brief.aspx

[8] Jared Bernstein and Jeff Chapman, *Income Picture,* Economic Policy Institute, September 26, 2003.

[9] Gene Koretz, "Economic Trends," *BusinessWeek*, March 12, 2001

[10] *Supporting America's Workers:* www.johnkerry.com/issues/workers/

Bush's Record

March and May 2004 and totaled almost 1 million. However, these gains did not reduce the unemployment rate of 5.6%. Still yet another statistic showed that real disposable income increased 4.3% in the first quarter of 2004; this compares to the 2.6% increase during all four quarters of 2003.

Q #1: How patriotic has President Bush been in making the median income of Americans a top priority of his economic policies?

- ❑ 4) Very Patriotic
- ❑ 3) Somewhat Patriotic
- ❑ 2) Neutral
- ❑ 1) Somewhat Unpatriotic
- ❑ 0) Very Unpatriotic

Kerry's Record

of responsibility of domestic programs from the federal to state governments. He still believes that states need flexibility and clear rules of accountability for results when taking over job training and employment programs that receive federal funding.[11]

Q#1: How patriotic has Senator Kerry been in making the median income of Americans a top priority of his economic policies?

- ❑ 4) Very Patriotic
- ❑ 3) Somewhat Patriotic
- ❑ 2) Neutral
- ❑ 1) Somewhat Unpatriotic
- ❑ 0) Very Unpatriotic

[11] John Kerry, *A Call To Service,* Viking, New York, NY, 2003, p. 72

Tax Cuts and Budget Deficits

> *"Tax relief is central to my plan to encourage economic growth, and we can proceed with tax relief without fear of budget deficits, even if the economy softens."*
> ~ George W. Bush, Western Michigan University, March 27, 2001

> *"The first and most important step we need to take to restore our common wealth is to restore fiscal discipline and the progressive principle of taxation. I want to repeal the Bush tax cuts targeted to the wealthiest Americans."*
> ~ John Kerry, A Call To Service, p. 73.

The topic of tax cuts and budget deficits is one of the more divisive issues separating the two primary presidential candidates.

While cutting taxes has been associated over the past 20 years with the GOP, even Democratic President Kennedy pushed through a tax cut, slashing the top marginal tax rate from 91% to 70%. He also reduced the lowest marginal tax rate from 20 to 14%. Keep in mind the budget deficit the Kennedy-Johnson Administration was dealing with was $36.5 billion in today's dollars.[12] Even after these cuts, the reduced tax rates were still far higher than contemporary tax rates on both rich and poor.

Republican Ronald Reagan was the first champion of major tax cuts, but Democratic President Bill Clinton enacted tax cuts, too (though he also increased the top marginal tax rate from 31 to 39.6% on incomes above $250,000). Clinton's middle class tax cut was modest, but his tax and other policies for the poor were the most generous of any president in history. Whereas Clinton inherited the largest federal deficits of any president, he left his successor with the largest budget surpluses in history.

Under President Bush, the 2003 deficit soared to $374.2 billion, twice that of 2002. The proposed FY 2005 budget is an estimated deficit of $541 billion, without including the costs for military operations and reconstruction of

[12] James Carville, *Had Enough? A Handbook for Fighting Back*, Simon & Schuster, New York, NY, p. 119.

Afghanistan and Iraq. To put that in perspective, next year's deficit will probably exceed the total federal budget of $600 billion proposed by Ronald Reagan in his first year as President.

A conservative organization, the Federalist Patriot (http://federalistpatriot.us/papers/04-07_paper.asp), views the emerging domestic fiscal crisis as an equally ominous threat to our national security as that of the al Qaeda terrorists. They believe that President Bush "has exhibited little leadership in fiscal restraint in his first term...Unmitigated government growth (and the resulting historic deficits) is the Bush administration's Achilles' heel in its bid for another term. Given the enormous growth of central-government spending under Republican-controlled executive and legislative branches, one is left to ponder if the tension created when those two branches are controlled by different parties is necessary to contain government growth."

To some conservatives, tax cuts are causing record deficits (borrowing) that will weaken the U.S., especially as interest rates rise. They believe it harms the U.S. to run high deficits when the same countries that are buying our debt, China and Japan, are the very ones we are negotiating with to reduce our trade deficit.

Others argue that tax cuts are finally turning the U.S. economy around, and that making these cuts permanent will send the right signals to investors and put more money into the pockets of every American. Tax cut proponents argue that citizens can do a better job of spending the money than government.

Q: Is it prudent to have tax cuts during record deficits?

President Bush's Record

President George W. Bush claims his tax cuts are responsible for the following accomplishments:

•The GDP growth rate of 6.1 percent in the last six months of 2003 was the fastest growth rate in nearly 20 years;

•U.S. household wealth hit a record high at the end of 2003, surpassing the previous peak set in the first quarter of 2000;

Senator Kerry's Record

Senator Kerry opposes the Bush Administration's current policies of combining tax cuts with large federal budget deficits. As President, he plans to cut the deficit in half. The Bush Administration claims Kerry has voted for tax increases 350 times over his 18-year Senate career. The Kerry campaign counters that his votes and record reflect policies aimed at providing greater wealth for the middle

Bush's Record

•Since 2001, the U.S. economy has grown more than twice as fast as the European Union and Japan.

The Bush Administration maintains that the vast majority of Americans are benefiting from the tax cuts, including 4 million poor people with children that will not have to pay any tax at all.

However, some Republicans are hesitant in making the Bush tax cuts permanent in light of estimates of a $477 billion federal deficit in the current fiscal year.[13] While President Bush has presided over the largest real increase in discretionary budget outlays in the last 40 years, recent memos obtained from the Office of Budget and Management suggest that steep cuts in popular programs will be necessary to reach budget deficit reduction targets beginning next year.[14]

Ironically enough, Bush is being criticized from conservatives who complain about increases in federal spending and from liberals, who argue his tax cuts have hit the disadvantaged too hard and have created large deficits. For example, the conservative Heritage Foundation claims government spending has exceeded $20,000 per household for the first time since World War II.[15]

Kerry's Record

and lower classes, the Americans that have suffered the most during the recent economic downturn.

Kerry disagrees with some in his own political party who argue that all of the Bush tax cuts should be repealed. He points out repealing these tax cuts would cost a middle-class family with two kids nearly $2,000.

Kerry's concerns for the majority of taxpayers are driven by the following fact: today's two-income family earns 75% more than its single-income counterpart a generation ago, but actually has less to spend due to soaring housing costs, day care, college tuition and health care. His proposed tax cuts are therefore targeted to make college and health care more affordable.

The tax cuts enacted by the Bush Administration account for 17 times as much of the current swing from federal budget surplus to deficit as have the Bush Administration's increases in discretionary spending. Kerry is not proposing the drastic reductions in popular federal programs that recent Bush Administration memos suggest. Instead, tax cuts earmarked for the top 1 percent of the wealthiest Americans would be eliminated, saving over $500 billion over the next 10 years, along with other tax cuts aimed at the well-to-do.[16]

---

[13] "Republican Senators Try To Hack At Deficit," *Reuters*, March 9, 2004.

[14] Paul Krugman, "Bush's Dooh Nibor Economics," New York Times News Service.

[15] Doug Bandlow, "A Conservative Case for Voting Democratic," *Fortune*, April 19, 2004.

[16] Committee for Tax Justice Fact Sheet, May 26, 2001: http://www.ctj.org/html/gwbfinal.htm.

Bush's Record

According to the math of non-partisan budget experts, the bulk of benefits from making the Bush tax cuts permanent will flow to the 20% of Americans who make over $200,000 annually. The four-fifths of Americans whose incomes are below $76,400 are likely to face tax increases or spending cuts that will substantially exceed the size of the tax cuts they receive.[17]

Q #2: Has President Bush been patriotic in his polices concerning tax cuts and budget deficits?

- ❑ 4) Very Patriotic
- ❑ 3) Somewhat Patriotic
- ❑ 2) Neutral
- ❑ 1) Somewhat Unpatriotic
- ❑ 0) Very Unpatriotic

Kerry's Record

Q #2: Has Senator Kerry been patriotic in his polices concerning tax cuts and budget deficits?

- ❑ 4) Very Patriotic
- ❑ 3) Somewhat Patriotic
- ❑ 2) Neutral
- ❑ 1) Somewhat Unpatriotic
- ❑ 0) Very Unpatriotic

[17] "No Free Lunch: When Tax Cuts Are Finally Paid For, Many Households Are Net Losers," Center on Budget and Policy Priorities, press release, June 2, 2004.

Corporate Accountability

> *"We will use the full weight of the law to expose and root out corruption. My administration will do everything in our power to end the days of cooking the books, shading the truth, and breaking our laws."* ~ George W. Bush, July 22, 2003

> *"Including Enron and other corporate meltdowns, the [Bush] Administration has presided over the worst corporate accountability crisis in living memory. This crisis has damaged not only millions of individual investors, but our economy as a whole."* ~ John Kerry, A Call To Service, p. 69

Among the promises to Americans expressed in the Preamble to the U.S. Constitution is the small phrase "to establish justice." This simple concept can be applied broadly, yet it does address a fundamental belief that in America, the federal government has an important role to play in ensuring that all workers are treated fairly in an open economy.

The issue of corporate accountability is a rather recent phenomenon. Our Founding Fathers lived in a time when the economy was dominated by agrarian society characterized by small farms and small businesses. The rise of the industrial revolution did bring the issue of the power of big business to the forefront.

It was a Republican – Teddy Roosevelt – who was among the first to give voice to concerns about curbing the power of private sector companies, once calling for a ban on campaign contributions to political campaigns.[18] He was particularly upset about those firms such as oil companies that profited from extracting the rich natural resource base of the young nation. The infamous "Robber Barons" of the late 19th century, who were known for the ruthless exploitation of people and land in pursuit of profit, helped shape his views on the need for the federal government to intervene into the marketplace. And it was another Roosevelt – Democrat Franklin D. Roosevelt – who expanded government's caretaker role even further with his New Deal programs.

---

[18] Paul Begala, *It's Still The Economy, Stupid,* Simon & Schuster, New York, NY, 2002, p. 79.

The issue of corporate accountability is a challenge for any contemporary President. The rights of companies to operate in a free and open market must be balanced against the rights of workers to a secure income and retirement package. The advent of globalization is only intensifying the debate over how best to govern corporations in a time of sweeping changes in employment trends and corporate social responsibilities.

Q: Is requiring corporate accountability a worthwhile American tradition?

President Bush's Record

Corporate scandals the likes of Enron, WorldCom, Tyco and others all occurred while current President Bush has been in office. The Enron scandal has particularly caused Bush political problems since Enron CEO Ken Lay has been George W. Bush's most generous political patron over his career, investing over $550,000 in campaign contributions.[19]

Among the concerns stemming from corporate scandals such as Enron is a loss of investor confidence in the all important power supply business, loss of retirement savings of employees, and lingering negative impacts upon the stock market.

On July 9th, 2001, the President's Corporate Fraud Task Force was created. According to the Bush Administration, this special task force has accomplished the following:[20]

• Obtained over 250 corporate fraud convictions or guilty pleas.

Senator Kerry's Record

Senator Kerry has pledged to close corporate loopholes that allow companies to pocket huge profits that Kerry instead wants to channel into tax relief for the middle class. He has also called for bigger budgets for the Securities and Exchange Commission to investigate corporate abuses of the public trust in order to restore investor confidence in the stock market and corporate America in general.[21]

Kerry also believes that corporate leaders have been granted too much protection when it comes to lucrative compensation packages that are honored while their companies may be struggling to keep workers on the payroll and paying back loans. Kerry has proposed to tighten the laws that allow corporations to take advantage of tax deductions for performance-based executive pay. He has also complained that contracts with WorldCom have increased by 600% since 2000, the year George W. Bush was elected to the presidency. Under a Kerry Administration, firms such as WorldCom that have been

[19] James Carville, *Had Enough? A Handbook for Fighting Back,* Simon & Schuster, New York, NY, 2003, p. 225.

[20] *One Year Anniversary of President Bush's Corporate Fraud Task Force:* www.georgewbush.com/Economy/read.aspx?ID=2002.

[21] *John Kerry Pledges to Close Corporate Loopholes,* September 15, 2002: www.johnkerry.com/pressroom/releases/archive/pr_2003_0915b.html.

Bush's Record

• Charged 354 defendants with some type of corporate fraud crime in connection with 169 filed cases;

• Investigated 500 companies involved with 320 suspected corporate fraud cases;

• Collected in excess of $85 million in restitution, fines and forfeitures.

Perhaps the highest profile investigation under Bush's tenure has been the controversy over the so-called "energy crisis" in California. Working with the Federal Energy Regulatory Commission, the Task Force has collected $35 million on behalf of energy consumers. However, critics contend that $40 billion in long-term power purchase contracts with the State of California should be nullified given the evidence of market manipulation by Enron and a long list of other power companies.

Kerry's Record

found guilty on charges of accounting fraud – or who are moving operations offshore – would be banned from receiving government service contracts.

Kerry has also proposed that companies should have to account for accounting discrepancies. He points to a recent report issued by the Joint Committee on Taxation that found Enron claimed a $2.3 billion profit between 1996 and 1999 in reports to investors, but reported a $3 billion tax loss to the IRS.

Bush's Record

Q #3: Has President Bush been a good patriot when it comes to the issue of ensuring corporate accountability?

- ❑ 4) Very Patriotic
- ❑ 3) Somewhat Patriotic
- ❑ 2) Neutral
- ❑ 1) Somewhat Unpatriotic
- ❑ 0) Very Unpatriotic

Kerry's Record

Q #3: Has Senator Kerry been a good patriot when it comes to the issue of ensuring corporate accountability?

- ❑ 4) Very Patriotic
- ❑ 3) Somewhat Patriotic
- ❑ 2) Neutral
- ❑ 1) Somewhat Unpatriotic
- ❑ 0) Very Unpatriotic

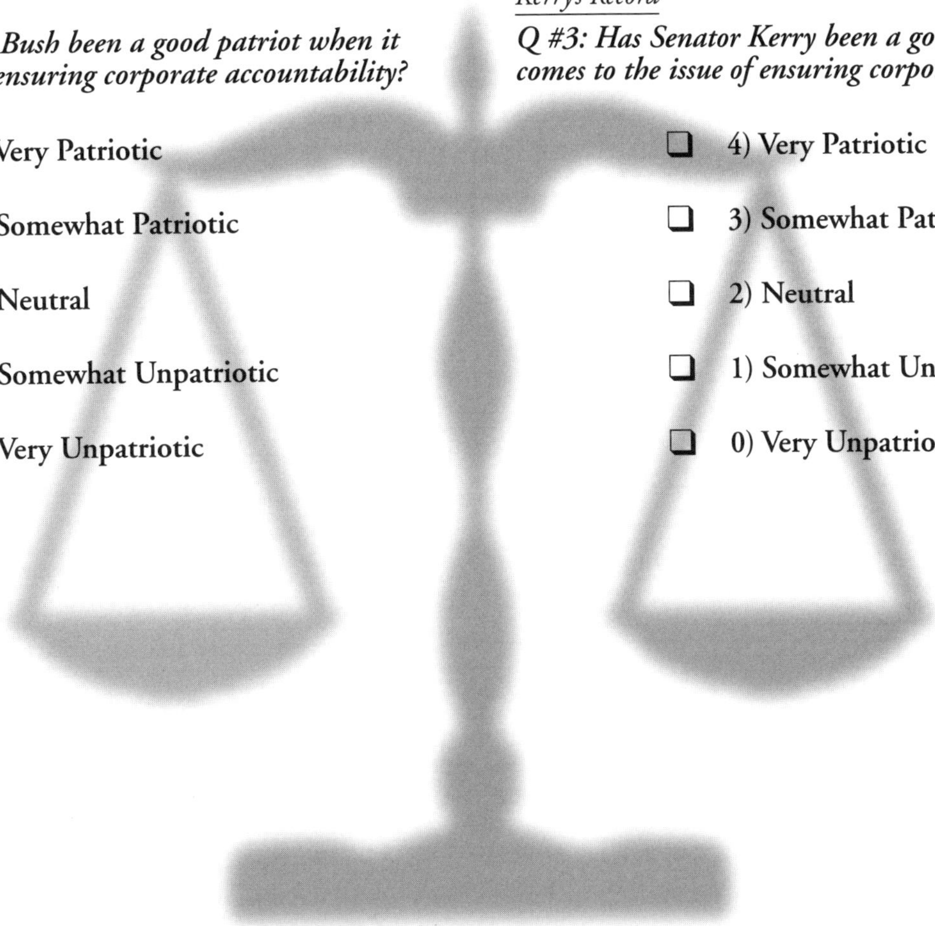

Social Security

"A rigid economy of the public contributions and absolute interdiction of all useless expenses will go far towards keeping the government honest and unoppressive." ~ Thomas Jefferson, letter to Lafayette, 1823

> *"Social security is the single most successful program in government history. [But] within two decades, there simply won't be enough younger workers to pay the benefits earned by the old. For those on social security-or close to receiving it-nothing will change. In my economic plan, more than $2 trillion of the federal surplus is locked away for social security. For years, politicians have dipped into the trust fund to pay for more spending. And I will stop it."*
> ~ **George W. Bush, Speech in Rancho Cucamonga May 15, 2000**

> *"Well, we did protect Social Security in the U.S. Senate, and Social Security is safe and sound well into the next two decades or more. With very minor changes, with a strong economy, the next generation will have Social Security. I will never privatize Social Security. I will never try to extend the retirement age for Social Security. And I will not cut any benefits for Social Security."*
> ~ **John Kerry Source: Democratic 2004 Presidential Primary Debate in Iowa January 4, 2004**

Democratic President Franklin D. Roosevelt signed into law the Social Security Act in 1935. The original law was to pay retirement benefits only to the primary worker of a family. That restriction was changed in 1939 to also pay benefits to survivors and retiree's spouse and children. Disability benefits were then added in 1956.

The next major modification to the law occurred in 1983 under Republican President Ronald Reagan. For the first time, half the population of Social Security recipients were being asked to pay income tax on payments if the payments totaled more than $34,000 in any one year. The rationale for this tax increase on former workers was to recapture money lost from payroll tax deductions given to companies.

How does Social Security work today? Depending on when a worker was born, federal benefits typically start at age 65 to age 67 – and sometimes as early age 62. Payouts depend on income history. A mathematical formula called the AIME (Average Indexed Monthly Earnings) calculates a citizen's Social Security payment. The basis for the amount of a Social Security payment is a worker's 35 years of highest earnings during which he or she paid Social Security tax, indexed with inflation and wage growth. Adding up the income accumulated during the 35 years and dividing by the number of months (420) yields a monthly average. Earnings subjected to the Social Security tax only apply to the first $80,000 or so that a worker earns per year, a figure that is changed from year to year depending on annual recalculations of average income and the cost of living.

Most workers' paychecks finance their Social Security "accounts" under the term "FICA" (Federal Insurance Contributions Act). These "accounts" operate more or less as an IOU from the federal government. This is the crux of the current controversy surrounding Social Security. Critics worry that annual surpluses in Social Security tax collections that most Americans assumed being used to build up a reserve for the "Baby Boomers" generation may be distressed to learn that these funds are currently being spent on other government programs or to reduce the government debt."[22] Today, the Social Security Trust Funds are essentially an accounting device to show how much the federal government has borrowed. The 2004 Social Security Trustees' Report projects that the fund will be "bankrupt" by 2018.[23] Perhaps a more accurate way to describe the dilemma is that the Social Security Trust Fund will be paying out more than it takes in, and either a reduction of benefit payment and/or increased taxes will need to make up the difference.

Reforming Social Security is very contentious issue. At stake are the retirement plans of U.S. citizens and the assumption that the federal government has a role to play in making our "golden years" more enjoyable by guaranteeing a

[22] Matthew Yglesias, "Think Again: Spinning Social Security," March 18, 2004, americanprogress.org

[23] The Heritage Foundation, "Social Security Basics," WebMemo #143, September 12, 2002

minimal amount of retirement income based on how much each of us – or our spouses and parents – worked most of their lives. Yet because the Social Security is so complex, a majority of Americans do not understand some of the nuances of proposed reforms by either presidential candidate or political party. A lack of straightforward information coming from both policy makers and politicians doesn't help the situation.

Based on our federal government's past record of prudence (or lack thereof) with taxpayer funds, growing numbers of senior citizens and Baby Boomers alike worry about whether they will ever receive the Social Security payments owed to them by the federal government. It is a moral issue of right and wrong that workers get back their own money.

Q: Is it patriotic to ensure that the Social Security program remain viable?

President Bush's Record

When first unveiled, President Bush's Social Security reform proposals largely skirted specifics. The basic thrust of his plan during the 2000 presidential campaign was to allow Americans to invest a portion of their Social Security funds into the stock market in order to earn a better rate of return. "Right now, the real return people get from what they put into social security is a dismal 2% a year," said Bush. "Over the long term, sound investments yield about a 6% return. American securities markets, over time, have been among the most reliable investments in the world. I trust Americans to manage their own money. Everyone should be a part-owner in the American dream."[24] Of course, this idea was floated before the stock market

[24] "Renewing America's Purpose" May 15, 2000, *New York Times*, p. A18.

[25] Speech at Massachusetts Democratic Convention May 31, 2002.

Senator Kerry's Record

Kerry has looked to history as he has contemplated the challenges associated with revitalizing the nation's Social Security program. "We must uphold the promise of Roosevelt, Truman, Kennedy, Johnson, Carter, and Clinton and never allow the President and his Republican friends to threaten Social Security by putting it on the Wall Street trading block," is how Kerry responded to President Bush's reform proposals.[25]

Kerry's votes in the Senate demonstrate that he has been consistent in his support for a Social Security "lockbox" and being opposed to any effort to privatize any portion of the Social Security program. In 1998, before the stock market meltdown, Kerry voted against an amendment

Bush's Record

cooled and investors lost confidence in what had been an incredible bull market – as well as a good portion of their retirement nest eggs.

The primary distinction between Bush and Gore on Social Security was Bush's support for making personal retirement accounts part of Social Security reform. Still, it was unclear, for instance, exactly how much money people could set aside for individual accounts and what sort of investment options they would have. But the lack of specifics on matters like what percentage of payroll tax would go to accounts, and what age group would see the change, opened Bush to charges that he was masking some of the hard choices ahead and trying to sidestep questions about how he could afford the transition. The cost of transition could be as much as $1 trillion.[26]

Here are the key principles guiding President Bush's Social Security policies:[27]

• We must not change Social Security for those now retired, or nearing retirement.

• All Social Security funds in the federal surplus must stay where they belong, dedicated to Social Security.

• The payroll tax must not be raised. We cannot tax our way to reform.

Kerry's Record

that had the Senate Finance Committee expressing its support for legislation to use the federal budget surplus to establish personal retirement accounts as a supplement to Social Security.[28] He also voted against an amendment that would have established an income tax deduction for Social Security taxes paid by employees and the self-employed.[29]

Kerry signed the manifesto, "A New Agenda for the New Decade." This manifesto points out that an ever-growing share of the federal budget today consists of automatic transfers from working Americans to retirees. The federal government already spends seven times as much on the elderly as it does on children. To allow that ratio to grow even more imbalanced would be grossly unfair to today's workers and future generations, argues the manifesto. Kerry endorses the position that Social Security needs to be modernized to reflect conditions not envisioned when they were created in the 1930's and the 1960's. Social Security, for example, needs a stronger basic benefit to bolster its critical role in reducing poverty in old age. Such a change, however, will only add to the cost of the Social Security programs unless they are accompanied by structural reforms that restrain their growth and limit

[26] *New York Times*, p. A18 May 16, 2000

[27] Speech in Rancho Cucamonga, in "Renewing America's Purpose" May 15, 2000

[28] S. Con.Res.86 ; vote number 1998-56 on April 1, 1998 www.senate.gov/legislative, U.S. Senate: Legistative and Records Home

[29] S. Con. Res 57 ; vote number 1996-140 on May 22, 1996 www.senate.gov/legislative, U.S. Senate: Legistative and Records Home

Bush's Record

• Reform should include personal retirement accounts for young people. A young worker can take some portion of his or her payroll tax and put it in a fund that invests in stocks and bonds. We will establish basic standards of safety and soundness, so that investments are only in steady, reliable funds. Money in this account could only be used for retirement, or passed along as an inheritance.

Among the pledges candidate Bush made during his campaign for president was to dedicate all Social Security money to Social Security, a so-called "lock box" approach that was being championed by his presidential candidate opponent Al Gore. As President, Bush has broken this pledge due to huge federal deficits. Bush has also suggested he might raise the age for being eligible for Social Security benefits as a way to help extend the life of the ailing program.[30]

Kerry's Record

their claim on the working families whose taxes support the programs.

By 2010, Kerry hopes to have accomplished the following goals as outlined in the Manifesto:

• Honor our commitment to seniors by ensuring the future solvency of Social Security

• Make structural reforms in Social Security that slow their future cost growth, modernize the benefits package, and give beneficiaries more choice and control over their retirement security.

• Create Retirement Savings Accounts to enable low-income Americans to save for their own retirement.

[30] CNN.com, "GOP Arizona Debates" November 22, 1999

Bush's Record

Q #4: How patriotic has President Bush been when it comes to keeping Social Security a viable federal government program?

❑ 4) Very Patriotic

❑ 3) Somewhat Patriotic

❑ 2) Neutral

❑ 1) Somewhat Unpatriotic

❑ 0) Very Unpatriotic

Kerry's Record

Q #4: How patriotic has Senator Kerry been when it comes to keeping Social Security a viable federal government program?

❑ 4) Very Patriotic

❑ 3) Somewhat Patriotic

❑ 2) Neutral

❑ 1) Somewhat Unpatriotic

❑ 0) Very Unpatriotic

The Disenfranchised

"If a free society cannot help the many who are poor, it cannot save the few who are rich." ~ John F. Kennedy, Inaugural Address, 1960

> *"And those of us who have been blessed with the opportunity to help must help save lives. The strength of America is found in the hearts and souls of our fellow citizens. This country must not fear the influence of faith in order to make America a better place."*
> **~ George W. Bush, New Orleans, Louisiana, January 14, 2004**

> *"President Bush speaks of compassion, but withholds commitment. It is time to demand more of our leadership and to answer the Americans who are asking to give more of themselves. It is time to renew the spirit of service and citizenship, of duty and patriotism that belongs to no one President and no one party, but should enlist all our people to do their part, in many different ways, to make our country better."*
> **~ John Kerry, Manchester, New Hampshire, May 19, 2003**

Addressing the needs of the disenfranchised – whether they are a minority child born into a low-income family or a low-income senior citizen who can no longer afford adequate health care – is among the most perplexing challenges facing any President of the United States. Despite the lofty ideals that America conveys to the rest of the world, the U.S. lags well behind the rest of the world when it comes to integrating the masses of immigrants and other financially challenged people into its economy. Yet at the same time, the U.S. still represents the opportunity of success in pursuit of happiness and the rest of the American Dream.

Among the charters given to us by our Founding Fathers was the order to "secure the blessings of liberty to ourselves and our posterity." There is no doubt that the U.S. remains a nation where anyone can strike it rich and build upon financial success with freedoms many Americans have come to take for granted. However, it is also true that the U.S. levels of poverty are unprecedented among developed nations. The gap between rich and poor is getting wider instead of closing since the turn of the century.

"A nation that continues year and year to spend more money on military defense than on programs of social uplift is approaching spiritual death." ~ Reverend Martin Luther King, New York City, April 4th, 1967

In Matthew 25, Jesus tells us the Christian community that all of the nations of the world will be judged at the end of history according to how they have responded to the needs of the poor and the oppressed:

"Come, you that are blessed by my Father, inherit the kingdom prepared for you from the foundation of the world; for I was hungry and you gave me food, I was thirsty and you gave me something to drink, I was a stranger and you welcomed me, I was naked and you gave me clothing, I was sick and you took care of me, I was in prison and you visited me. Then the righteous will answer him, Lord, when was it that we saw you hungry and gave you food, or thirsty and gave you something to drink? And when was it we saw you're a stranger and welcomed you or naked and gave you clothing? And when was it that we saw you sick or in prison and visited you. And the king will answer them, Truly I tell you, just as you did it to one of the least of these who are members of my family, you did it to me." (Matthew 25:34-40)

Consider the following facts in light of Reverend Martin Luther King and the Bible:

• Of the 30 countries known as the Organization for Economic Cooperation and Development (OCED) that produce two-thirds of the world's economic activity, only Mexico has a lower tax burden than the U.S. The average American sees roughly 22% of his or her income going to federal, state and local taxes. In comparison, in Sweden, over 50% of income goes to pay for government services.[31]

• Of major industrialized nations, the U.S. spends the least per capita to assist low-income citizens. For every dollar we Americans pay to help out the disenfranchised, the people of Norway invest $70.[32]

---

[31] James Carville, *Had Enough? A Handbook for Fighting Back*, Simon & Schuster, New York, NY, 2003, p. 115.
[32] Tony Campolo, "Is America Losing Its Soul?," *Spiritual Perspectives on America's Role as a Superpower*, SkyLight Paths Publishing, Woodstock, Vermont, 2003, p. 76

•At 10.7%, the U.S. poverty rate is more than twice the average of the 19 wealthiest countries in the world. Most other developed nations spend between 7 to 10% of their GDP on social transfers to the disenfranchised. In contrast, the U.S. spends roughly 4%.[33]

•The proportion of the adult population living in relative poverty is more than twice as high in the U.S. as in France, Germany or Italy (19% versus 8%). Approximately 25% of U.S. children now also live in poverty.[34]

Some economists argue that pay inequality in the U.S. actually provides greater incentives for Americans to improve themselves through creating their own businesses or in obtaining a higher degree of education in order to land a better paying job. Yet even these economists acknowledge that the benefits of pay inequality during the past decade have been captured by those further up on the income scale.

Q: Should Jesus' example of compassion influence our national policy toward the poor, the homeless and forgotten people in our society?

President Bush's Record

President Bush has made the issue of "compassion" a centerpiece of his Administration's attempt to help lift more Americans up out of poverty. He has also taken the controversial stance to allow faith-based organizations to compete for federal dollars to run and manage federally funded programs for low-income and chronically poor Americans.

One of Bush's first official actions as President was to create the White House Office of Faith-Based and

Senator Kerry's Record

Senator Kerry has been consistent in his votes supporting programs for minorities that are often among the most disenfranchised Americans. He supports both set-asides of federal procurement contracts with minorities and minority set-asides for education loans. Kerry also supports what he calls "full immigration reform."[35]

Kerry's positions are quite similar to former Democratic President Bill Clinton. He voted for the Clinton Administration's welfare reform and like Clinton,

[33] Gene Koretz, Economic Trends:...and the Home of the Poor, Business Week Online, March 12, 2001.
[34] Peter Singer, *The President of Good and Evil: The Ethics of George W. Bush*, Dutton Books: The Penguin Group, New York, NY.
[35] Julie Cortez, "Seven Questions for Massachusetts Senator John Kerry," *El Hispanic News*, May 26, 2004.

Bush's Record

Community Initiatives. The purpose of this new office is to remove barriers for religious organizations seeking federal funding to aid the disenfranchised. As of January 2004, the federal Housing and Urban Development Department had distributed $168 million to 600 different faith organizations to help provide housing for the homeless.[36]

Despite efforts to fight poverty, the basic measure of the depth of poverty was greater in 2002 than any other year on record going back to 1979.[37] The Bush Administration also cites the "No Child Left Behind" as one of its programs based on compassion. However, this program based on federal standard tests has never been fully funded and so far appears to have failed to live up to its lofty-sounding moniker.

The U.S. government has also traditionally played a major role in helping the poor, starving and disenfranchised around the globe. Education assistance for Africa doubled to $265 million between 2001 and 2004, assisting 12.5 million children to go to school who otherwise would be deprived of a basic education.[38] The

Kerry's Record

advocates a shift away from traditional affirmative action programs over the long-term. His past votes align with moderate Democrats attempting to move beyond New Deal policies of the past and toward a new economic system that valued self-reliance. In 1992, Kerry warned his alma mater at Yale University about a "culture of dependency." He added, "We must ask whether [social disintegration] is the result of a massive shift in the psychology of our nation that some argue grew out of the excesses of the 1960's, a shift from self-reliance to indulgence and dependence, from caring to self-indulgence, from public accountability to public abdication and chaos."[39]

Many of Kerry's positions also align with his Catholic faith. He supports increasing the minimum wage and aligning future increases to inflation. He supports the reunification of immigrant families and the restoration of benefits for legal immigrants. He supports subsidized housing programs for the poor. All of these positions can be considered in line with Catholic beliefs about being compassionate for those in America who have less, but

[36] President Bush speech delivered at the Union Bethel AME Church in New Orleans, Louisiana on January 15, 2004: http://www.georgewbush.com/Compassion/read.aspx?ID=2165.

[37] Global Action on Aging, *Poverty Increases and Median Income Declines for the Second Consecutive Year,* Center on Budget and Policy Priorities, September 29, 2003: www.globalaging.org/elderrights/us/medianincome.htm.

[38] *Issue Brief: The President's Compassion Agenda*, www.georgewbush.com/Compassion/Brief.aspx.

[39] Socialist Worker Online, *The Many Faces of John Kerry,* February 6, 2004.

Bush's Record

Bush Administration has also launched the Emergency Plan for AIDS Relief, a $15 billion international effort to "turn the tide in the global effort to combat HIV/AIDS."

Q #5: How compassionate has President Bush been on addressing the need of America's disenfranchised?

- ❑ **4) Very Compassionate**
- ❑ **3) Somewhat Compassionate**
- ❑ **2) Neutral**
- ❑ **1) Somewhat Uncompassionate**
- ❑ **0) Very Uncompassionate**

Kerry's Record

who are, nonetheless, seeking life, liberty and the pursuit of happiness.[40]

Q #5: How compassionate has Senator Kerry been on addressing the need of America's disenfranchised?

- ❑ **4) Very Compassionate**
- ❑ **3) Somewhat Compassionate**
- ❑ **2) Neutral**
- ❑ **1) Somewhat Uncompassionate**
- ❑ **0) Very Uncompassionate**

[40] Joan Chittister, "Is John Kerry a Good Catholic?", *National Catholic Reporter*, May 12, 2004.

CHAPTER 2

Homeland & National Security

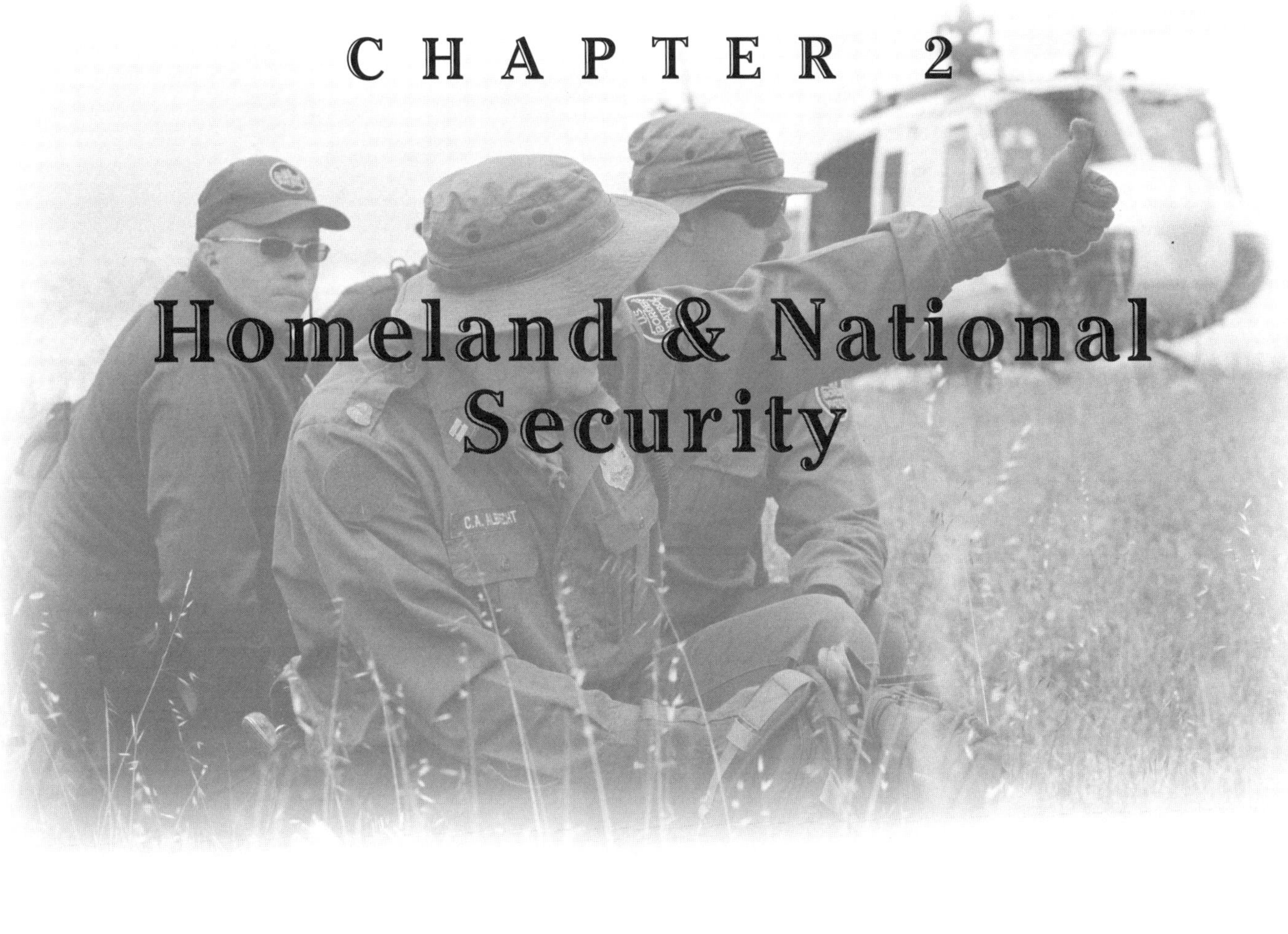

INTRODUCTION

Protection of our interests is a national right and obligation. As expressed in our Constitution, the federal government is charged with providing "for the common defense." Every nation has a right to protect itself from foreign aggression, though there is considerable disagreement about how best to provide that protection. For centuries, many governments maintained huge military forces to implement their international policies, both to guard their own borders and to exercise influence beyond those borders.

Until recently, having a large military translated into a high degree of self-protection because nations would go to war against one another by sending armadas of ships or planes loaded with soldiers to invade the other country. Such large-scale mobilizations were expensive undertakings that could wipe out a nation's treasury, so they were not engaged in lightly.

Today, the landscape of war has changed. Instead of soldiers dug into lines of trenches, trading gun and cannon fire over hundreds of yards of open field, a handful of helicopters go in to enemy territory for a surgical strike. Instead of the Japanese sending a fleet of warships and planes to attack Pearl Harbor, a small terrorist organization sent 19 of its members to hijack four passenger jets and fly them into buildings on our own native soil.

Now we face an even greater threat, but from a smaller force. With suitcase nukes (as they are so benignly referred to), a single person could theoretically detonate a nuclear warhead into New York City, killing hundreds of thousands of people, and contaminating one of the world's centers of commerce for decades to come.[1]

The U.S. military budget now exceeds $420.7 billion and yet many Americans still worry about the next seemingly inevitable terrorist attack.[2] That allocation of federal funding amounts to roughly a sixth of our federal government budget. And that's just for the Pentagon. Additional costs of our national security include tens of billions of dollars

[1] Stephen Schwartz, "The Case For Suitcase Nukes," www.FrontpageMagazine.com, April 13, 2004.

[2] Anup Shah, www.globalissues.org, April 4, 2004.

for the Central Intelligence Agency (CIA), and other intelligence operations, and many billions more in "defense" expenditures hidden in other budget line items.[3]

Americans have always been willing to invest their tax dollars in national defense. Unfortunately, these investments often escape scrutiny. Estimates of waste from the overlap of the four major branches of the military exceed $30 billion a year.[4] Then there is the so-called "Black Budget," estimated to be costing taxpayers approximately $35 billion a year. These Pentagon investments include planning for new technologies to be used in World War III and World War IV. The Black Budget programs receive minimal oversight from a select few people at the very highest levels of government.

The 9/11 attack, coupled with the misreading of cues on weapons of mass destruction being hidden in Iraq, are now considered to be the two "gravest dysfunctions" in the national security apparatus of the U.S. since the creation of the CIA at the dawn of the Cold War.[5]

In response to the terrorist attacks in 2001, the government merged 22 smaller federal agencies into one big Department of Homeland Security (DHS). With a current budget of $33.5 billion, DHS was designed to protect Americans from terrorist threats both foreign and domestic. Its color-coded threat level chart is perhaps the most visible impact this new federal agency has had on our lives.

The key concern with national and homeland security is whether a half-trillion dollars a year investment in military measures can be truly effective in protecting our country. Our nation's borders are still quite porous. Thousands of people arrive illegally in the U.S. every day. America is a center for world commerce, with only cursory controls placed on the myriad ships and planes and trucks that cross our borders daily.

Spending as much as we do on national and homeland security will never offer U.S. citizens complete protection. In such a free and open society as the U.S., it is simply not plausible to spend enough tax dollars to ever achieve complete security. So the critical issues regarding national and homeland security are whether the current approach to providing that security is right – and whether the resources being invested in that effort are adequate to do the job.

---

[3] Michael E. Salla, *The Black Budget Report*, Center for Global Peace at American University, Washington, DC, November 23, 2003 www.american.edu/salla/

[4] Mark Zepezauer and Arthur Naiman, *Take The Rich Off Welfare*, Odonian Press, 1996.

[5] Todd S. Purdam, "Analysis: Politics, Washington Mind-Set Work Against Reform," *New York Times*, July 23, 2004.

Budgeting for Homeland Security

> *"The reality is, vast oceans can no longer protect us, and therefore we must have, and we do have, a clear strategy to defend our homeland. Oh, we'll do everything we can to prevent attacks on America. As we do so, we'll reduce our vulnerabilities and prepare for any attack that might come; that's our duty; that is our collective mission."*
> ~ George W. Bush, Washington, DC, March 2, 2004

> *"We deserve a president of the United States that doesn't make homeland security a photo opportunity and the rhetoric of a campaign. We deserve a president that makes America safer."*
> ~ John Kerry, Seattle, Washington, May 26, 2004

Most Americans would agree that funding for national and homeland security should be a high budget priority. If the nation is unsafe, all of our other tax expenditures could be jeopardized. But spending money and buying security is not necessarily the same thing. For decades, national security experts have debated whether the U.S. military was prepared to fight the last war. Our military operations in Vietnam and Iraq underscore the dangers of war. Even possessing the vast resources of the U.S.– and the most powerful military force on the planet – does not always assure a clear and quick total victory.

U.S. policy makers may need to better define what security is. For example, does our definition of security extend beyond our physical boundaries and if so, how far and under what circumstances? Second, we as a nation must decide if there is not a more effective way to achieve security. For example, negotiations may prove to be a better investment than maintaining an enormously expensive military and relying upon the threat of retaliation. Third, we must decide how much we are willing to spend on preparedness, realizing that we can never be prepared for every eventuality.

Consider, too, that it is apparently not too difficult to bring contraband into the U.S. Millions of dollars in illegal drugs penetrate our borders every day, despite billions spent to stop this flow. Would it be more difficult to bring in illegal drugs or containers of anthrax? The fact that no arrests were made in the anthrax mailings of 2001 underscores the steep challenge facing our domestic agencies in trying to make America secure again.

We need homeland security, but does merging several federal departments and spending billions of dollars provide the assurance we want? At present, each taxpayer is spending roughly $3,900 on the military and $290 for homeland security every year.[6] Are we getting our money's worth? Do you feel safer for spending that amount of money on national and homeland security?

Q: Should funding homeland security be a high budget priority?

President Bush's Record

President Bush touts the USA Patriot Act as proof that he understands the risks Americans now face in the 21st century. Having created the DHS and initiated more than a dozen different programs designed to help Americans feel more secure, President Bush gives the impression of a leader committed to homeland security.

The Bush Administration has improved airport security by authorizing the hiring of more than 50,000 freshly trained federal screeners at airports, granted the U.S. Coast Guard 700 high-speed vessels to protect our ports, and signed into law Project BioShield, which provides the drug industry with incentives to develop bioterrorism vaccines and antidotes.[7]

Yet the cost effectiveness of the Bush Administration's approach has been questioned. The non-partisan 9/11 Commission has documented that flat budgets, an outdated structure, and bureaucratic rivalries all contributed to the massive intelligence failures regarding the 9/11 attack

Senator Kerry's Record

Senator Kerry has supported the Bush Administration in voting for the Patriot Act, but has criticized President Bush and his GOP colleagues in Washington DC for not fully funding a number of promising initiatives that he claims will reduce both the threat of a terrorist attacks and allow communities to better respond after such an attack has occurred.

The key components of Senator Kerry's approach to funding Homeland Security are as follows:[8]

• Enlist the National Guard to be trained to serve as key personnel in the event of a terrorist attack. The National Guard would both help communities set up and execute security procedures and protocols as well as help evacuate and quarantine people, if necessary.

• Expand Americorps to help make the U.S. more secure. Since the 9/11 attack, applications to join Americorps have doubled, but funding for this government program was cut in half by Congressional Republicans.

---

[6] The White House, President Bush's Fiscal Year 2005 Budget, February 2, 2004.

[7] Deb Reichman, "Shielding Americans From Bioterrorism", *Associated Press*, July 21, 2004; Protecting the American People: http www.georgewbush.com/HomelandSecurity/Brief.aspx.

[8] Plan To Make America Stronger and Safer: www.johnkerry.com/issues/homeland/plan.html.

Bush's Record

and subsequent invasion of Iraq.[9] An apparent lack of coordination between the new DHS and the Federal Bureau of Investigations (FBI), the Justice Department as well as other security agencies has now been clearly documented. The 9/11 Commission staff report found that there was "no credible evidence that Iraq and al Qaeda cooperated on attacks against the United States."[10] There have been no high level firings for any of these failures. George Tenet, Director of the CIA did resign, but for "family reasons".

In his book, *Against All Enemies*, former counter-terrorism czar Richard Clarke wrote: "Regrettably, the Administration sought to do homeland security on the cheap, telling [Department of Homeland Security Secretary] Tom Ridge that creating the new department had to be 'revenue neutral,' jargon for no new money to implement the largest government reorganization in history."[11] Nearly 4 out of 5 city mayors have reported funding shortfalls that have prevented them from developing efficient terrorist threat detection or emergency preparedness systems.[12] The Maritime Transportation Act of 2002, signed into law by President Bush, could

Kerry's Record

Senator Kerry has proposed to expand the mission of Americorps to include homeland security in order to utilize its members to help out on emergency medical response teams and other functions.

• Create a new Community Defense Service akin to the Civil Defense Program that operated during World War II. In the words of the Kerry campaign, Volunteer Service Captains would act "as a 21st Century Neighborhood Watch program," with local citizens becoming much more involved in the day-to-day monitoring and planning for terrorist attacks.

• The final part of Senator's Kerry's "Defend America" Initiative would call upon the private sector to integrate new communication and other technologies into America's effort to combat terrorism.

Along with adding more personnel and integrating the expertise of the new technologies into America's effort to strengthen homeland security, Senator Kerry is also pushing for common federal standards that would help local governments determine what they need to do in order to respond to chemical, biological and other forms of terrorist attacks.

---

[9] Edward Epstein, "U.S. Safer – But Not Safe, 9/11 Commission Says; Indictment: Report Assails Intelligence, Government Failures," *San Francisco Chronicle*, July 23, 2004, p. 1.

[10] Philip Shenon, "9/11 Report Expected To Dismiss al Qaeda, Iraq Link," *New York Times*, July 12, 2004.

[11] Richard Clarke, *Against All Enemies: Inside America's War on Terror,* Free Press/Simon & Schuster, New York, NY, 2004.

[12] Plan to Make America Stronger and Safer: http://johnkerry.com/issues/homleand/plan.html.

Bush's Record

play a key role in the fight against terrorism since 95% of non-North American trade moves through a handful of U.S. ports. The measure focuses on bolstering the physical security systems at ports. Since 9/11, funding to implement new security systems has increased by $200 to $300 million, an amount critics maintain is not adequate to make a difference in securing our ports from terrorist attacks.[13]

Q #6: How patriotic has President Bush been in budgeting for homeland security?

- ❑ **4) Very Patriotic**
- ❑ **3) Somewhat Patriotic**
- ❑ **2) Neutral**
- ❑ **1) Somewhat Unpatriotic**
- ❑ **0) Very Unpatriotic**

Kerry's Record

In addition, Kerry believes that domestic intelligence agencies need to be reformed. He has criticized the Bush Administration's reliance upon the FBI to play a lead role in domestic surveillance in light of its historic mission to catch and prosecute criminals. Senator Kerry prefers creating a new and independent federal intelligence agency dedicated solely on gathering domestic intelligence.[14] This idea has been subsequently endorsed by the 9/11 Commission.

Q #6: How patriotic has Senator Kerry been in his budgeting for homeland security?

- ❑ **4) Very Patriotic**
- ❑ **3) Somewhat Patriotic**
- ❑ **2) Neutral**
- ❑ **1) Somewhat Unpatriotic**
- ❑ **0) Very Unpatriotic**

[13] Defending Our Skies, Sea and Land: http://johnkerry.com/issues/homeland/plan.html.
[14] Reforming Domestic Intelligence: www.johnkerry.com/issues/homeland/plan.html.

The Patriot Act

"Key elements of the Patriot Act are set to expire next year. Some politicians in Washington act as if the threat to America will also expire on that schedule. Yet we have seen what the terrorists intend for us, in deadly attacks from Bali to Mombassa to Madrid. And we will not forget the lessons of September the 11th. To abandon the Patriot Act would deprive law enforcement and intelligence officers of needed tools in the war on terror, and demonstrate willful blindness to a continuing threat."
~ George W. Bush, Washington, DC, April 17, 2004

"The problem with the Patriot Act are two words: John Ashcroft. If we had an attorney general of the United States who respected the Constitution, there's no reason in the world that you can't do the things necessary. I will change the Patriot Act. And we had the good common sense, may I add, to put in the Patriot Act a sunset clause so it dies automatically at the end of this year and we'll change it."
~ John Kerry, Milwaukee, Wisconsin, February 15, 2004

In the emotional upheaval and political chaos that followed the terrorist attacks of September 11, 2001, President Bush pushed through Congress legislation that gave the Executive Office vast new powers to watch, investigate and detain suspected terrorists without the traditional constitutional safeguards that have long been treasured in our nation, and respected as fundamental principles of freedom here and abroad for more than two hundred years.

The USA Patriot Act, which passed through Congress without being closely examined in legislative committees, gave the Justice Department extraordinary powers to dig into the private lives of all U.S. citizens without the legal protections provided in the past.[15] The checks and balances that would normally make sure people still had their Constitutional rights were suspended by the Patriot Act. The rationale was that we were involved in a new kind of war where our cherished freedoms had to be sacrificed in order to bolster our national security.

[15] CBSNews, "Congressional Opponents Lash Out At Patriot Act, Ashcroft," September 23, 2003.

Though the Patriot Act passed both houses by wide margins, there were members on both sides of the aisle who had serious questions about the legality of the act. The Patriot Act gave unprecedented (and perhaps unconstitutional) powers to federal authorities to investigate Americans and other people residing within our borders. Some conservatives and liberals alike balked at some of the provisions, charging that abuse of the powers granted in the legislation could transform the U.S. into something more resembling a police state than the land of the free and home of the brave.[16]

While everyone understood the fear and anger that drove the legislation, while everyone wanted to feel safer and to track down those who had helped the 9/11 terrorists – and particularly to prevent a re-occurrence – few Americans realized how the Patriot Act would be used by the Department of Homeland Security and other federal agencies in matters that have nothing to do with terrorism. Civil liberties experts argue that the laws on the books were adequate to address the terrorist threat, before and after 9/11. The problem was not one of laws, but one of intelligence and execution by the FBI, CIA and other intelligence agencies.[17]

The chief criticisms of the USA Patriot Act lodged by its opponents are that its broad surveillance and intelligence powers are being abused. Instead of focusing on going after bona fide terrorists, the Justice Department has been using powers granted by the Patriot Act to fight Oregon's assisted suicide law, close down marijuana co-ops serving chemotherapy patients in California, and subpoena abortion records from hospitals and clinics across the country.

While many Christians and other Americans might support these efforts to address issues of morality, the Patriot Act was sold to lawmakers and citizens alike as a measure needed to fight terrorism. Given the limited resources of the current federal government, critics contend that the resources earmarked to make America safer are instead being used unlawfully. Is closing down co-ops selling marijuana authorized by a state ballot initiative more important than fighting terrorism?[18]

---

[16] Kelly Patricia O Meara, "Police State", www.insightmag.com, November 9, 2001.

[17] Henry J. Waters III, "FBI, CIA Report: Who is to Blame?", *Columbia Daily Tribune*, June 13, 2004.

[18] Dean Baker, *The Cost of the War on Terrorism And the Cost of Social Security*, Center for Economic and Policy Research, February 1, 2002 http://cepr.net.

Q: Has the Patriot Act been successful in apprehending terrorists?

President Bush's Record

The key question is whether the Patriot Act has clearly reduced the risk of another terrorist attack? The Bush Administration claims the following success stories:[19]

- Six members of an alleged terror cell in Portland, Oregon planning to attack Jewish schools or synagogues were arrested and convicted as they sought to travel to Afghanistan and fight U.S. forces there;
- Libardo Florez-Gomez, who was suspected of laundering over $1 million a month to a leftist rebel group in Colombia, was successfully prosecuted;
- Rajib Mitra was sentenced to eight years in prison for using a computer to jam the Madison, Wisconsin's radio system 22 times in 2003;
- An individual who in 2002 sent more than 200 threatening letters containing white powder to government agencies, businesses and individuals in Louisiana was convicted after law enforcement was able to tap Internet and phone records from a cable company that would not have been possible absent the Patriot Act.

Accompanying these few examples of success have been several reported abuses. For example, the Justice

Senator Kerry's Record

Senator Kerry has said that he wants to retool the Patriot Act and/or enact new laws that protect Americans from terrorists while also protecting our civil liberties. He has also promised to appoint an Attorney General that agrees with these principles.

Like most Democrats and Republicans in Congress, Kerry voted for The Patriot Act. Today, Senator Kerry feels that some provisions of the law need to be strengthened (such as the language addressing money laundering), while others need to be narrowed in order to protect people's civil liberties (such as the library "sneak-and-peek" search provisions).[20] In essence, Kerry is proposing to fine-tune the Patriot Act in order to make America more secure, while responding to critics in both political parties worried that the Patriot Act is being misused by federal government agents pursuing a divisive hidden political agenda.

Senator Kerry is calling for more judicial oversight over enforcement agencies relying upon the Patriot Act.[21] For example, Kerry would still allow "sneak-and-peek" searches by law enforcement – as long as a judge approves the continuing need for such secret searches. When it comes

[19] Dan Eggen (The Washington Post), Chronicle News services and Associated Press, "Ashcroft Defends Patriot Act as Effective," *San Francisco Chronicle,* July 14, 2004, p. A13.

[20] Guard Liberty At Home: http://www.johnkerry.com/issues/homleand_security/homeland_plan.html

[21] "Bush Ad Falsely Implies Kerry Would Repeal Wiretaps of Terrorists," FactCheck.org, June 1, 2004.

Bush's Record

Department incarcerated Jose Padilla two years ago, claiming he was a terrorist operating at the behest of al Qaeda. A high Pentagon official claimed to have evidence that Padilla was planning to detonate a "dirty bomb" but there was no indication that Padilla had the wherewithal to make any kind of bomb.[22]

The federal State Department now issues a report every year on terrorist activity. The first such report was released in 2003, trumpeting how the Patriot Act, DHS and other Bush Administration initiatives had made great progress against reducing the terrorist threat. However, the report contained major errors in fact. Secretary of State Colin Powell apologized for the report, which he blamed on clerical errors. The errors were not small. Indeed, one of the mistakes understated the number of terrorist attacks by half.

While an updated version was subsequently released, questions remain. Skeptics contend the State Department may have been massaging the data to make the Bush Administration's war on terrorism appear more successful than it actually was. The revised report showed that 625 people died in terrorist attacks in 2003, not 307 as previously reported. Terrorist incidents deemed "significant" were the highest in 2003 since 1982, when government first began tracking acts of terrorism.[23]

Kerry's Record

to wiretaps, Kerry has urged adding "adequate checks (and) safeguards" against eavesdropping on persons other than the authorized target, the same restrictions on roving wiretaps included in the current criminal code.

Interestingly enough, conservative Republicans worried about violations of 4th Amendment rights share Kerry's concern about the Patriot Act infringing upon civil liberties. Even President Bush's campaign chairman Marc Racicot has conceded that the Patriot Act could use "refinement…so that it does not end up invading the civil rights of any American."[24] Other Patriot Act critics include Free Congress Foundation President Paul M. Weyrich, former Virginia Governor James S. Gilmore III, American Conservative Union Chairman David A. Keene and Republican Senator Larry Craig of Idaho. Craig is the lead Senate sponsor of the "Security and Freedom Ensured Act (S. 1709)," a measure that would implement Kerry's suggested amendments. The legislation has four Republican co-sponsors: Michael Crapo of Idaho; Lisa Murkowski of Alaska; Arlen Specter of Pennsylvania and John Sununu of New Hampshire.

[22] Brigid O'Neil, *Jose Padilla: A Constitutional Challenge for Us All*, The Independent Institute, December 18, 2003: www.independent.org.

[23] Mike Nartker, "Revised 2003 Terrorism Report Doubles Death Count," Global Security Newswire, June 23, 2004: www.nti.org/d_newswire issues/2004_6_23.html

[24] Marc Racicot, Remarks at News Conference at Arab American Institute National Leadership Conference, Dearborn, Michigan, October 17, 2003.

Bush's Record

Q #7: How patriotic has President Bush been in reducing the terrorist threat with the Patriot Act?

- ❑ 4) Very Patriotic
- ❑ 3) Somewhat Patriotic
- ❑ 2) Neutral
- ❑ 1) Somewhat Unpatriotic
- ❑ 0) Very Unpatriotic

Kerry's Record

Q #7: How patriotic has Senator Kerry been in reducing the terrorist threat with the Patriot Act?

- ❑ 4) Very Patriotic
- ❑ 3) Somewhat Patriotic
- ❑ 2) Neutral
- ❑ 1) Somewhat Unpatriotic
- ❑ 0) Very Unpatriotic

Pre-Emptive Attacks

> *"The liberation of Iraq is a crucial advance in the campaign against terror. We've removed an ally of al Qaeda, and cut off a source of terrorist funding. And this much is certain: No terrorist network will gain weapons of mass destruction from the Iraqi regime, because the regime is no more."*
> ~ George W. Bush, Aboard USS Lincoln, May 1, 2003

> *"In giving the President this authority, I expect him to fulfill the commitments he has made to the American people in recent days–to work with the United Nations Security Council to adopt a new resolution setting out tough and immediate inspection requirements, and to act with our allies at our side if we have to disarm Saddam Hussein by force. If he fails to do so, I will be among the first to speak out."*
> ~ John F. Kerry, U.S. Senate, October 9, 2002

The very idea that the U.S. would attack a foreign nation without that nation first declaring war against us disturbs more than a few Americans given our country's history of ending – not starting – wars. But these people were in the minority. They perceived the pre-emptive strike in Iraq as a moral issue without precedent in U.S. history. Yet the majority of American citizens were propelled by fear and anger generated by the terrorist attacks of September 11th, 2001 and supported the invasion of Iraq with patriotic fervor.

Most people initially found the attack on Iraq as a necessary shift in public policy given these uncertain times of terrorism and shifting modes of war. However, as the war has dragged on, as no weapons of mass destruction have been found, as no Iraqi links to al Qaeda have been established, and as the sordid images of the prison torture sink in, many early supporters of the war are having second thoughts. A CBS/New York Times poll conducted between July 11-15, 2004 revealed that 37% of Americans approved of how President Bush has handled the situation in Iraq, while 58% disapproved. Five percent were undecided.[25]

To avenge the terrorist attacks, we first invaded Afghanistan to eradicate the Taliban regime and to eliminate the al Qaeda training camps that the Taliban allowed to exist. But the main thrust of the response to the 9/11 terrorist

[25] www.pollingreport.com/iraq.htm

attacks was the invasion of Iraq. The White House, using the bully pulpit, charged that Saddam Hussein was working with al Qaeda and claimed that Iraq presented an imminent threat to use weapons of mass destruction against the United States.[26] Citing what turned out to be unverified evidence of a weapons stockpile, President Bush persuaded Congress to give him the authority to invade Iraq and then tried to cajole the United Nations to support the U.S. plans.

The United Nations, the majority of the world's nations, as well as the majority of the world's people, all opposed the invasion. While they agreed that Saddam was a terrible dictator, they were unconvinced of charges that he was connected to the 9/11 terrorists or was ready to strike the U.S. with weapons of mass destruction. The U.S. went ahead with the attack. Subsequently, it became clear that the "proof" of weapons of mass destruction that the president has delivered in his 2003 State of the Union Address, and that Secretary of State Colin Powell had asserted to the United Nations the following month, was unsubstantiated.

It also turned out that the Administration had been planning to invade Iraq well before the 9/11 terrorist attack.[27] Speculation about the reason for the attack have ranged all over the map. Some claimed it represented an over-arching neo-conservative political strategy for the Middle East based, in part, on some interpretations of the Bible. Another reason may have been to secure petroleum sources. Yet another was to avenge the purported plan to assassinate President Bush's father in Kuwait a decade earlier. Ironically enough, our president's father – George Bush, Sr. – had been emphatic about the U.S. not invading Iraq.[28]

After the failure to capture Osama Bin Laden, some analysts are advocating a different approach. They believe international cooperation and more funding for the International Police (Interpol) could be more effective than military attacks on terrorist targets.

War is the ultimate power of a government. A pre-emptive attack to combat terrorism may be able to be justified in today's dangerous world. In order to keep its legitimacy, however, the evidence justifying such a radical departure from past U.S. public policy needs to be clear, convincing and shared with the American people.

---

[26] Center For American Progress, "In Their Own Words: Iraq's 'Imminent' Threat," January 29, 2004.

[27] Ron Suskind, *The Price of Loyalty*, Simon & Schuster, New York, NY, 2004: http://theprice ofloyalty.ronsuskind.com/thebushfiles/.

[28] George H.W. Bush and Brent Scowcroft, "Why We Didn't Remove Saddam," www.millat.com, March 2, 1998.

Q: Is a pre-emptive strike to combat terrorism patriotic?

President Bush Record

Top Bush Administration officials were planning to invade Iraq just after President Bush took office in January of 2001. That was in January, eight months before the terrorist attacks of 9/11. Paul O'Neill, the former Treasury Secretary in the Bush Administration, said in Ron Suskind's book, *The Price of Loyalty,* that he was aware of planning for the invasion of Iraq in the very first few days of the Bush Administration.

In his book, *Against All Enemies: Inside America's War on Terror,* former counter-terrorism czar Richard Clarke also made it clear that President Bush was focused on Iraq after the 9/11 attacks, even though Clarke repeatedly told him that there was no connection between Iraq and the terrorists. He said the president insisted that Clarke "find" a link, although as he reported, there was no link that could be fully substantiated by the variety of intelligence agencies seeking such evidence.

There is no question that President Bush would have had support of the American people if he had launched a preemptive attack against the terrorists in advance of the 9/11 terrorist attack, just as Democratic President Franklin D. Roosevelt would have been lauded for attacking Japan if he had done so before Pearl Harbor. But such is 20/20 hindsight. President Bush can hardly be faulted for not

Senator Kerry's Record

Senator John Kerry voted to give the president the authority to invade Iraq, pending conditions such as the U.N. inspectors completing their work and the U.S. garnering the support of its allies. His support for the resolution was based on the "evidence" presented by President Bush. Like most Americans, Senator Kerry believed President Bush when he warned that Iraq was an imminent threat to the United States. Senator Kerry has since been roundly criticized for endorsing the Iraq invasion plan– even with his reservations – by some in his own Democratic Party.

Was the pre-emptive invasion of Iraq justified? Kerry has said no, though he recently stated that he would not rule out a pre-emptive strike in the future if he had adequate intelligence of a threat.[29] Senator Kerry has expressed concern about the considerable destabilization of our relations with allies in Europe, such as France and Germany, and the influx of foreign terrorists into Iraq as reasons why the invasion was a mistake.

While Kerry now believes the invasion of Iraq was a mistake, he has never said that he regretted his vote. Indeed, he has stood firm on the principle of protecting the U.S.: "This is my message to terrorists: As commander in chief, I will bring the full force of our nation's power

[29] Ken Guggenheim, "Kerry Says He'd OK Pre-Emptive Strike," *Associated Press*, July 17, 2004.

Bush's Record

engaging in a pre-emptive attack on terrorists such as Osma bin Laden since such terrorists are not traditional targets. Unlike traditional targets, al Qaeda lacks a country or a headquarters in a city or other location. Indeed, terrorists such as al Qaeda purposively hide, scattering themselves throughout a variety of countries, continually relocating to avoid detection.

So when the U.S. invaded Iraq, it was on the basis of what we now know to be false premises. According to the report by the non-partisan 9/11 Commission, a series of assumptions about Iraq proved to be wrong:[30]

• No clear link between Saddam Hussein and Osama bin Laden has been discovered;

• No weapons of mass destruction were stockpiled in Iraq;

• There was no threat of an imminent attack by Iraq on the U.S.

Kerry's Record

to bear on finding and crushing your networks. We'll use every resource of our power to destroy you." He went on to say that if it ever seemed that the country was under imminent threat, "As commander in chief, I will do whatever is necessary to stop it."[31]

Sharing responsibility (and the burden and the risk) is the only way to gain new military and financial commitments in Iraq. That's how Senator Kerry views the evolving situation today. His solution to the Iraq situation is three-fold: (1) make Iraq a part of NATO's Global Mission; (2) authorize a High Commissioner for Governance and Reconstruction; and (3) launch a massive effort to build an Iraqi security force.

[30] David E. Sanger and Robin Toner, Bush Insists on Iraq-al Qaeda Link, New York Times wire story published in the *San Francisco Chronicle*, June 18, 2004; Philip Shenon, "9/11 Report Expected To Dismiss al Qaeda, Iraq Link," New York Times wire story published in *San Francisco Chronicle*, July 12, 2004, p. A6.

[31] Senator John Kerry, Seattle Speech, May 27, 2004.

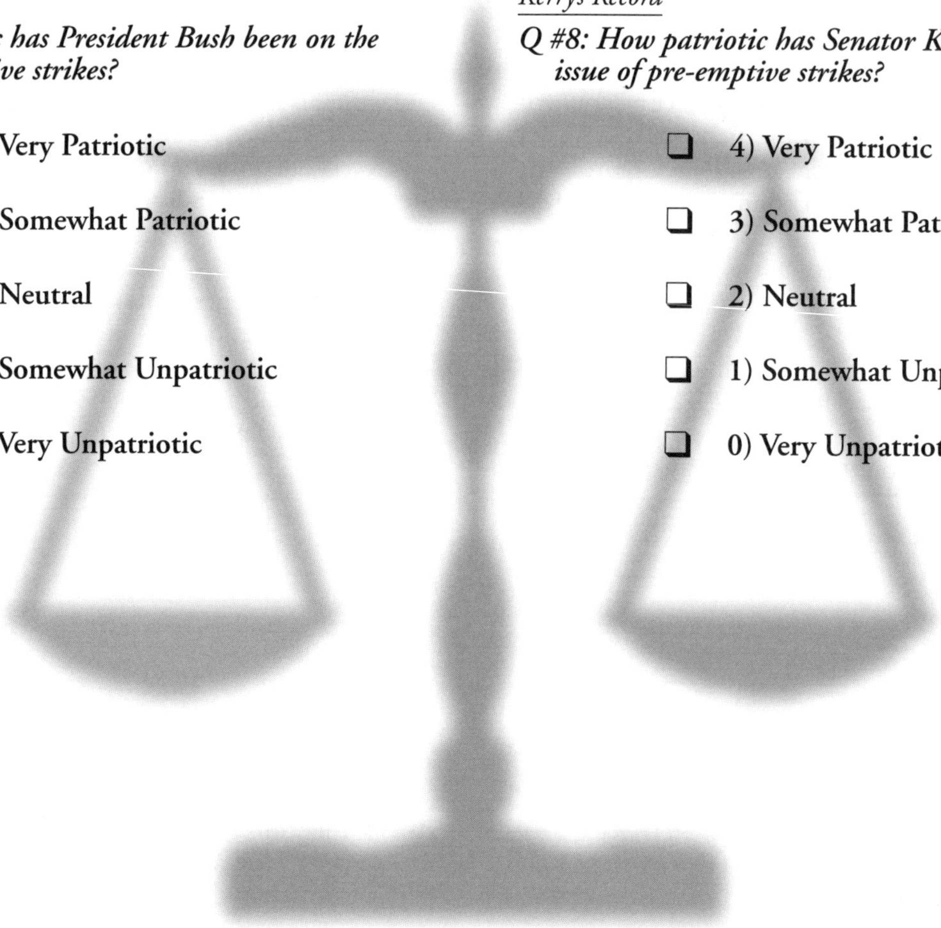

Bush's Record

Q #8: How patriotic has President Bush been on the issue of pre-emptive strikes?

- ❑ 4) Very Patriotic
- ❑ 3) Somewhat Patriotic
- ❑ 2) Neutral
- ❑ 1) Somewhat Unpatriotic
- ❑ 0) Very Unpatriotic

Kerry's Record

Q #8: How patriotic has Senator Kerry been on the issue of pre-emptive strikes?

- ❑ 4) Very Patriotic
- ❑ 3) Somewhat Patriotic
- ❑ 2) Neutral
- ❑ 1) Somewhat Unpatriotic
- ❑ 0) Very Unpatriotic

Biological and Chemical Weapons

> *"The greatest threat before humanity today is the possibility of secret and sudden attack with chemical or biological . . . weapons."*
> ~ George W. Bush, National Defense University, February 11, 2004.

> *"As president, I will tackle this issue head-on, . . . work(ing) with other countries to . . . stop the development of chemical and biological arsenals."*
> ~ John Kerry, Portsmouth New Hampshire, December 17, 2003.

A familiar image from the War for Independence is red-coated British troops, marching in rows of muskets while Patriot farmers fire at them from behind trees and stone fences. Formal conventions of warfare of the time pitted confronting armies on an open battlefield. These 'rules of engagement' were followed by America for nearly 150 years.

World War One brought changes to the waging of war. The mechanical age brought aircraft, tanks, and submarines. Bombs and missiles were launched upon soldiers and civilians. Both biological and chemical weapons entered modern warfare.[32]

Military leaders tend to use the available technology to win a war. New weapons, however, often confront the strategists with difficult moral issues. This was especially true for biological and chemical weapons.

The first use of chemical weapons in World War I occurred April 22, 1915, when Germany released chlorine gas into the battlefield of Ypres, Belgium. Two years later, Germany launched mustard gas attacks. By the war's end the death toll from chemical weapons approached 100,000 people. This initial use of chemical and biological weapons was so

[32] Ivan Vorobyov, "Evolution of Wars and Armed Conflicts of the 20th Century", *Military Thought*, January 2002.

inhuman, that The Geneva Protocol prohibiting their use in war was negotiated in 1925. The United States signed the Protocol, but failed to ratify the entire treaty.

Little else was done until after World War II. Chemical and biological weapons continued to be developed in great secrecy by nations throughout the 50's, 60's and 70's. International pressure mounted for new stronger treaties to curb such weapons.

On November 25, 1969, President Nixon unilaterally renounced the use of biological weapons in war by the United States, and restricted research to immunization and safety efforts. In 1972 The Biological and Toxin Weapons Convention entered into full force, banning the production and stockpiling of these weapons. On January 22,1975 the United States ratified both this weapons convention and, finally, the 1925 Geneva Protocol. Our moral leadership as a nation was evident. Chemical, biological and toxin weapons were unacceptable in a civilized society.

However, almost as soon as the Conventions were affirmed, Iraq used chemical weapons in its war against Iran as well as Kurdish dissidents - the first use of chemical weapons in combat since World War I. As a result, President Reagan's administration presented an international treaty to ban production and storage of chemical weapons. The concern over the use of such weapons during the Persian Gulf War increased support for the treaty. Once again, on May 13, 1991 President George H.W. Bush announced that the United States renounced the use of chemical weapons for any reason. Our moral position and a patriotic one, was reinforced in January 1993 when we signed the Convention.

Despite the efforts to make biological, chemical and toxin weapons morally repugnant and legally impermissible among nations, terrorists found the weapons useful. On March 20, 1995, Sarin nerve gas released into the Tokyo Subway by terrorists killed 12 people and injured more than 5,000. Two years later, the Chemical Weapons Convention went into effect, with more than 160 signatories and 65 ratifications.[33]

Considering the volatility of today's world, a single individual with a bottle of nerve gas could wipe out hundreds of thousands of people, make vital areas of the planet uninhabitable for decades and destroy the global economy. Only by eliminating chemical, biological and toxin weapons together will the world ever be safe from such an attack.

---

[33] *The chronology of chemical and biological weapons* comes from Congressional Quarterly Researcher, at http://cqpress.com/context articles/cqr_chemical_chronology.html

Q: Would our national security be improved by working to halt the proliferation of biological and chemical weapons worldwide?

President Bush's Record

President Bush refused to apply the model Chemical Weapons Convention, developed by his father, to the grave threat of biological arms. The Convention prohibits the development, production, stockpiling or use of biological weapons.

In July of 2001, the Bush administration announced that it would not endorse a verification and monitoring protocol, which would require all signatories to submit to international inspections to ensure compliance.[34]

In September 2001, the New York Times reported on several secret U.S. bio-defense projects, including an attempt to build a bio-bomb, create a super-strain of anthrax, and construct a bio-weapons lab out of commercially available material.[35]

Activities endorsed by the Bush Administration include an attempt by the CIA to replicate a Soviet-designed cluster bomb intended to deliver biological weapons, and the Defense Intelligence Agency research into genetically

Senator Kerry's Record

Senator Kerry has called for a global effort to remove weapons-usable materials from the more than 100 insecure civilian plants around the world that still use this kind of material. And he has promised that he will appoint a top-level coordinator whose job is to make sure this gets done.

"Even though there is a very real threat of biological weapons in any one of the millions of containers which come into this country every year, there is no global system for tracking and security," Kerry has pointed out. "We have affordable, existing technology to detect whether they contain dangerous chemicals. As President, I would move immediately to protect American ports and the Americans who live near them by putting such a system in place."[36]

Senator Kerry voted YES on banning chemical weapons, a resolution ratified in 1997, as the Chemical (comprehensive) Weapons (convention) Ban (Senate Resolution 75).[37] The Senate approved the convention, although it added conditions regarding U.S. compliance

[34] *World Policy Journal*, Volume XX, No. 2, Summer 2003.

[35] Judith Miller, Stephen Engelberg, and William Broad, "U.S. Germ Warfare Research Pushes Treaty Limits," *New York Times*, September 14,2001.

[36] Speech by Senator John Kerry in Portsmouth, New Hampshire on December 17, 2003.

[37] "John Kerry on Homeland Security," On The Issues, 2004: http://www.johnkerry.com.

Bush's Record

engineered strains of anthrax spores for use as weapons. The Biological Weapons Convention requires signatories to make annual declarations of such research, and Washington has never listed these programs in its reports.[38]

Q #9: How patriotic has President Bush been on working to halt the proliferation of biological and chemical weapons worldwide?

- ❑ 4) Very Patriotic
- ❑ 3) Somewhat Patriotic
- ❑ 2) Neutral
- ❑ 1) Somewhat Unpatriotic
- ❑ 0) Very Unpatriotic

Kerry's Record

with inspections that have been cited as a precedent by other countries seeking to limit scrutiny.

Q #9: How patriotic has Senator Kerry been on working to halt the proliferation of biological and chemical weapons worldwide?

- ❑ 4) Very Patriotic
- ❑ 3) Somewhat Patriotic
- ❑ 2) Neutral
- ❑ 1) Somewhat Unpatriotic
- ❑ 0) Very Unpatriotic

[38] Phil Gasper, "The U.S. Develops New Weapons of Mass Destruction," *International Socialist Review*, Jan/Feb 2003.

Energy Security and Independence

"We lead the world in new technologies when it comes to energy, and we not only can find new ways of producing energy and make sure we do it in an efficient way, we make sure we can do it in a clean way . . . We lead the world in technologies to make production of energy cleaner so therefore I'm confident in predicting to the American people not only can we promote job security and increase jobs, but we can do so in a way that protects our environment. And I believe we have a duty to do so. I believe a responsible nation is one that protects the environment."
~ George W. Bush, Detroit Edison Monroe Plant, September 15, 2003.

"The sooner that we commit America to the science and discovery of renewable alternatives, the better off America will be, the better our health will be, the more effective our economy would be, the better our national security will be, and the better world citizen we will be. We need to commit ourselves to energy independence now."
~ John F. Kerry, New York, New York, September 25, 2003.

Independence has been a hallmark of American values and goals from the very beginning. In the early days of this country, slaves, horses and other animals, wood, water, and wind provided mechanical power. The invention of practical uses for steam power and electricity brought a shift toward fossil fuels as prime sources of energy. Later, the internal combustion engine created a massive industry that began consuming more and more oil.

Yet it wasn't until the oil embargo of 1974, and the long lines at gas filling stations, that America seriously turned its attention to a long-term strategy to achieve energy independence. U.S. programs developed in response to this "energy crisis" helped sire the world's renewable energy industry and the first U.S. fuel efficiency standards for motor vehicles.

The U.S. holds only 3% of the world's total oil reserves. Yet, today the U.S. consumes an estimated 20 million barrels of oil a month. Most of it goes into our gas tanks, but it is ubiquitous in contemporary life. You find petroleum in many chemicals, medicines, synthetic fabrics and almost everything plastic. We now import 11 million barrels of that oil at rising costs. Roughly a quarter of our balance of trade deficit is due to our purchase of foreign oil.

For more than a century, U.S. foreign policy has been affected in large part by petroleum. Over time, our national security strategies have become focused more and more on where petroleum is located geographically and which countries are pumping it out of the ground. Because much of the world's oil production comes from nations that are culturally and politically different from our own, the U.S. is caught between an insatiable demand for energy sources and being dependent on countries that are unfriendly to the U.S.

Our choices are not simple and they must address domestic reserves. Though the U.S. still has untapped reserves, growing numbers of prime sites are in environmentally sensitive areas. Even if we suspended all environmental protections, even if we could extract every drop beneath us, we would not produce enough to meet our own energy needs in the long term.

The only practical solutions are energy independence and alternative energy sources. At present, the vast majority of new power plants burn natural gas, the cleanest fossil fuel. The U.S. is now looking to import liquefied natural gas (LNG) from other countries. However, recent fears about terrorist attacks have stalled or killed LNG projects on East and West Coasts. We also need to find energy that will power our vehicles and industry without polluting and increasing our dependence upon foreign oil. The environment can no longer be sacrificed.

Efforts to develop a National Energy Strategy have yielded some progress in freeing new technologies to enter the marketplace and increasing our reliance upon domestic energy sources. Yet our transmission grid is still 1950s technology. Solar and wind power technologies, birthed in the U.S., provide less than 1% of the nation's electricity.

Q: Is it in our national interest to seek energy security and independence?

President Bush's Record

Hailing from Texas, Bush is quite familiar with the oil and natural gas businesses. Bush made tapping domestic fossil fuel sources a centerpiece of his National Energy Strategy.

Senator Kerry's Record

Senator Kerry has been among the staunchest congressional opponents of opening up Alaska National Wildlife Refuge to oil drilling.[39] So far, Kerry and his colleagues are prevailing. Kerry has also called for

[39] H. Josef Hebert, "Republicans Fail To Get Alaska Refuge Drilling Measure, By the Narrowest of Margins," *Associated Press*, March 19, 2003.

Bush's Record

Accessing oil supplies located below the National Arctic Wildlife Refuge in Alaska was a top priority for President Bush.[40] According to the United States Geologic Survey (USGS), the amount of oil in this area would supply America's oil needs for 6-18 months, maximum.

Reviving America's nuclear power industry is a key part of President Bush's proposed energy strategy. Nuclear power plants can generate substantial amounts of power round-the-clock without emitting any direct air emissions contributing to acid rain, urban smog and global climate change. Still, the U.S. has not built a new nuclear power plant in more than 20 years. Among the reasons is the lack of a safe, permanent repository for nuclear wastes. The Bush Administration has authorized construction of the Yucca Mountain, NV nuclear waste site.[41]

As Texas Governor, Bush signed into law a Renewable Portfolio Standard that is hailed by the U.S. wind industry as a model. The Federal Energy Regulatory Commission has been criticized for it's policing of the California and West Coast market in 2000-2001, but is praised by

Kerry's Record

continuing a moratorium on all oil drilling in the Outer Continental Shelf, as well as off the New England, Florida and California coasts.[42]

The bottom line for John Kerry is that we cannot drill our way to independence from foreign oil since the U.S. only possesses 3% of the world's total oil reserves.

Kerry has also consistently voted against federal approval of the Yucca Mountain nuclear waste repository.[43] Among his reasons are national security concerns about concentrating the nation's nuclear waste shipments to a single site.

Kerry also opposes the Bush Administration's proposal to revive the nation's nuclear power industry with new subsidies. Since nuclear power requires the largest subsidy of any electricity source, Kerry prefers to rely upon domestic renewable sources and efficiency.

Kerry agrees with the Bush Administration that a federal production tax credit should be extended to wind power, the lowest cost renewable energy option. Senator John Kerry has yet to take a position on an offshore wind

---

[40] "Bush Energy Plan Sent to Congress," *Environmental News Network*, June 29, 2001; "Norton Wants Energy Bill Veto If No ANWR Drilling," *Reuters*, September 19, 2002.

[41] Alison Mitchell, "Senate Approves Nuclear Waste Site in Nevada Mountain," *New York Times*, July 10, 2002.

[42] 103rd Congress, S. 2019, Senate vote 120, May 18, 1994; 107th Congress, House Resolution 2217, Senate vote 231, July 12, 2001.

[43] 105th Congress, S. 104, Senate vote 42, April 15, 1997; 106th Co ngress, S. 1287, Senate vote 8, February 10, 2000; 107th Congress, Senate Resolution 34, Senate vote 167, July 9, 2002.

Bush's Record

the wind power industry for its efforts on transmission scheduling and planning.

In his own words, this is how President Bush sums up his views on federal energy policy: "I support a comprehensive and balanced national energy policy. I do not believe, however, that the government should impose on power plants mandatory emissions reductions for carbon dioxide, which is not a "pollutant" under the Clean Air Act. Including caps on carbon dioxide emissions as part of a multiple emissions strategy would lead to an even more dramatic shift from coal to natural gas for electric power generation and significantly higher electricity prices. This is especially true given the incomplete state of scientific knowledge of the causes of, and solutions to, global climate change and the lack of commercially available technologies for removing and storing carbon dioxide."[44]

Kerry's Record

project proposed off of Cape Cod. Many residents there worry about scenic values as well as the lack of a coherent federal policy governing this emerging opportunity to harness some of America's most cost effective domestic energy sources.

Kerry has also called for raising mileage requirements on cars and Sports Utility Vehicles from the current 24 miles per gallon (mpg) to 36 mpg, claiming this simple increase in efficiency could reduce our oil consumption by 10%. He also wants to eliminate the so-called "SUV loophole" that allows businesses to write off up to $100,000 if they purchase these gas-guzzling vehicles. Kerry wants to encourage the use of hybrid vehicles and have the government invest in alternative energy research and development, seeking to draw 20% of our energy from renewable fuels by 2020.[45]

---

[44] Speech by George W. Bush, Washington, DC, March 15, 2001

[45] Energy Independence: www.johnkerry.com.

Bush's Record

Q #10: How patriotic has President Bush been in his efforts to move America toward energy security and independence?

- ❑ 4) Very Patriotic
- ❑ 3) Somewhat Patriotic
- ❑ 2) Neutral
- ❑ 1) Somewhat Unpatriotic
- ❑ 0) Very Unpatriotic

Kerry's Record

Q #10: How patriotic has Senator Kerry been in his efforts to move America toward energy security and independence?

- ❑ 4) Very Patriotic
- ❑ 3) Somewhat Patriotic
- ❑ 2) Neutral
- ❑ 1) Somewhat Unpatriotic
- ❑ 0) Very Unpatriotic

CHAPTER 3

Foreign Policy

INTRODUCTION

"A politician thinks of the next election. A statesman thinks of the next generation." ~ James Freeman Clark, American Clergyman[1]

Nowhere does the definition of patriotism – as a zealous defense of our country's interests – come into play more than in American foreign policy. At the founding of our nation, both idealism and realism, isolationism and interventionism (both unilateral and cooperative), interplayed with historical circumstances to create a unique foreign policy perspective.

The Puritans arrived on these shores to build the city on the Hill. In their view, salvation was grounded in religious freedom. From this religious vision grew the idealism of a God-given law of nations, a moral vision to govern the relationship of nations. Our idealism embraced freedom and peace, as God and Christ proclaimed them.

But we were also realistic. Our Founding Fathers did not want to be a colony nor become a colonial power. Self-interest as much as religious idealism guided the Founding Fathers. Our Constitution, grounded not in imperialism but democratic sentiments, is appropriately vague concerning the way foreign policy addresses our country's best interests.

The Founding Fathers were concerned about establishing a nation among nations. We needed to consolidate our rule of the North American continent. The vastness of the geography gave us the opportunity to live up to the ideals. George Washington, as he left office, cautioned our new nation to adopt an idealistic isolationism of few permanent foreign entanglements.

Throughout our foreign policy history we have adopted a variety of combinations of the attributes. In the 19th Century, The Monroe Doctrine validated our expansionist needs in America. We were ready to be the guardian of the Americas. Newspaperman John L. O'Sullivan coined the term Manifest Destiny. He said, "It was the right of our manifest destiny to overspread and to possess the whole of the continent for the great experiment of liberty . . ."[2] Our foreign affairs reflected our nation-building at home.

By the early 20th century, our foreign policy drifted toward international involvement. At the time, our largely military support of commercial interests was

[1] http://AmericanDiplomacy.org.

[2] Howard Jones, *The Course of American Diplomacy* (New York: Franklin Watts, Inc., 1985), p. 126. (The history in this chapter draws on Jones' work.).

grounded in our democratic and humanitarian motives. Republican President Theodore Roosevelt exemplified the realism of the times with his image of America talking softly and carrying a big stick.

Democratic President Wilson worked toward a diplomacy of idealism and peace. His administration accepted that entering World War I was a patriotic necessity to preserve American interests. However at the end of that first World War, America retreated once again into an isolationist foreign policy.

The Great Depression and World War II required American foreign policy to consider the responsibilities that come with international involvement. Once again, the foreign policy pendulum swung toward realistic intervention. It continued after the Second World War, in the Marshall Plan, the United Nations, and more. Our policing role in Korea, the Cold War and Vietnam were part of that change in perspective. American foreign policy had evolved into a pragmatic, flexible patriotic response to international affairs.

For most of the past half century, the rest of the world has craved the flexible continuity of American foreign policy. Whatever stresses may have existed between any administration and its domestic critics, most nations offer thanks that America has served the world as a voice of freedom and stability.

Nevertheless, some diplomats around the world are thinking differently in 2004. We are embroiled in hot spots including Afghanistan, Iraq, and the search for peace in the Middle East. Many traditional allies worry that America now disdains international organizations. American leaders reply that small member states express antagonism and opposition to genuine international interests and U.S. efforts. Our present reluctance to embrace international treaties and a willingness to alter or abrogate those we have historically supported, troubles other nations and even some of our most faithful allies.

Many of our own citizens believe our foreign policy is on the wrong track. And many nations no longer see America as the moral champion of liberty and self-determination. Still, America remains the unquestioned military power in the world. Our economic might is unrivaled.

The foreign policy issues now facing America are different from those America previously faced. Nationalism is on the rise and militant Islamists threaten us. Peace still eludes us. We live in an interdependent world, and both a moral and effective foreign policy is necessary. The patriot's responsibility is to find the best standing in international relations, lifting up our historical ideals, and recognizing our pragmatic needs.

International Law

As America's ideals of justice under law have inspired the world, international law, the Geneva Conventions, and the Universal Declaration of Human Rights, have come to reflect our nation's assumption of the intrinsic value of the human person.

"America cannot keep the peace alone. We must work closely with our friends and allies. I have worked to build bridges of personal diplomacy . . . America's foreign policy should respect and nurture our traditional alliances throughout the world and strengthen relations with countries in our own neighborhood . . . Ours should not be the paternalistic leadership of an arrogant big brother, but the inviting and welcoming leadership of a great and noble nation . . ."
~ George W. Bush, *A Charge to Keep*, p. 240, 1999

Americans deserve principled diplomacy . . . backed by undoubted military might . . . based on enlightened self-interest, not the zero-sum logic of power politics, . . . a diplomacy that commits America to lead the world toward liberty and prosperity. A bold progressive internationalism focuses not just on the immediate and imminent, but on insidious dangers that can mount over the next years and decade. The dangers span the spectrum from the denial of democracy, to destructive weapons, endemic poverty and epidemic disease. These are not just issues of international order, but vital issues of our own national security.
~ John Kerry, Quotations: www.johnkerry.com/issues/foreignpolicy

America's Founding Fathers urged our country to avoid entangling alliances with other nations. The Constitution specifically charges the U.S. Senate to approve all treaties and international agreements. The Bill of Rights and the Declaration of Independence speak of "inalienable rights" which all people share, because these are endowed by their Creator.

Over the past 230 years or so, America's understanding of inalienable rights has expanded to cover the rights of people from all racial backgrounds and from both sexes. As America's ideals of justice under law have inspired the world, international law, the Geneva Conventions, and the Universal Declaration of Human Rights, have come to reflect our nation's assumption of the intrinsic value of the human person. This benevolent and uplifting influence on the community of nations has largely been the result of our nation's religious roots. From this perspective, to abide by and support International Law is also to support the democratic ideals that America has championed.

President Bush has said, "Our commitment to democracy is tested in the Middle East. In many nations of the Middle East democracy has not yet taken root. And the questions arise: Are the peoples of the Middle East somehow beyond the reach of liberty? Are millions of men and women and children condemned by history or culture to live in despotism? Are they alone never to know freedom, and never even to have a choice in the matter? ... Every person has the ability and the right to be free."[3]

Despite this historic movement toward respect for all nations and all individuals, our government has fallen short of the ideal. Disavowed treaty obligations have set America on a course of independence and non-cooperation with the community of nations. This position has been considered necessary because other nations would not support America's international objectives.

It was rationalized that America should not entrust its security to other nations. It similarly chose to disavow the Geneva Convention in its treatment of prisoners because "enemy combatants" should not receive the rights of freedom. Detention camps were constructed and combatants, considered dangerous, were locked up and isolated without access to the protections which international law has historically guaranteed.

Q: Is it patriotic for American government to follow established principles of international law in the establishment of its foreign policy?

President Bush's Record

As Governor of Texas, George W. Bush demonstrated some trouble abiding by International Law. In a 1998

Senator Kerry's Record

Like a majority of lawmakers in Congress, Senator John Kerry voted to support the war in Iraq. Since then

3 President George W. Bush, November 2003, "Remarks at the 20th Anniversary of the National Endowment for Democracy", U.S. Chamber of Commerce, Washington, D.C., November 2003.

Bush's Record

report, "Lethal Justice," Amnesty International stated that "at every step in the death penalty process in the Texas state government, a litany of grossly inadequate legal procedures failed to meet recognized minimum international standards for the protection of human rights."

Amnesty International blamed the U.S. for the sustained erosion of human rights and international law. The non-profit organization claimed recent human rights abuses are currently the worst in 50 years. "Sacrificing human rights in the name of security at home, turning a blind eye to abuses abroad, and using preemptive military force when and where it chooses, have neither increased security nor ensured liberty."[4]

"The President of the United States is not bound by international laws prohibiting torture in the war against terror, and government agents who might torment prisoners at his direction, could not be prosecuted by the U.S. Justice Department." This advice was part of a classified report on interrogation methods prepared for Defense Secretary Donald Rumsfeld in March 2003, after commanders at Guantanamo Bay in Cuba complained that they were not getting enough information from prisoners."[5]

The Bush administration chose not to grant Geneva Convention rights to prisoners in Guantanamo Bay and other secret detention centers.

Kerry's Record

Kerry has become critical of President Bush and his strategy, espousing instead a view he deems "progressive internationalism." This means that he was not against the War in Iraq if they were a threat to the U.S. Also, Kerry was against the "go it alone" strategy the Bush Administration used to carry out the attack. Kerry has promised that if elected president, he would "go to the United Nations and travel to our traditional allies to affirm that the United States has rejoined the community of nations."[6]

Kerry has said he speaks from a position of strength on international issues and hopes to return to the multilateral cooperative tradition of democratic internationalism forged in the course of two world wars and the Cold War. From this vantage point, multilateral organizations are vehicles for the promotion of our ideals and the protection of our interests around the world. Senator Kerry claims to recognize that the ideals and interests of these democratic internationalists are consistent with the peace, prosperity, and self-determination of all countries around the world.

Democratic internationalists purport to understand that there are times when America must challenge the UN, NATO, and our allies to stand up for our own preferred values here in the U.S. And they also claim to realize that there are times when America must be challenged to live up to its values as well. "Today, America has taken a rare

[4] Saul Landau, "Amnesty International Report", *Z Magazine*, June 18, 2004.

[5] "Defense Department Report", The Wall Street Journal (via the *New Delhi Hindu*), June 7, 2004.

[6] Kenneth R. Timmerman, "Kerry Will Abandon War on Terror," Insightmag.com.

Bush's Record

Critics contend the unilateral act of pre-emptive strike, invasion, and occupation of Iraq are all considered as acting against International Law."[7]

Q #11: How patriotic has President Bush been in honoring and following principles of international law?

- ❑ **4) Very Patriotic**
- ❑ **3) Somewhat Patriotic**
- ❑ **2) Neutral**
- ❑ **1) Somewhat Unpatriotic**
- ❑ **0) Very Unpatriotic**

Kerry's Record

step in human history in arguing that its national interests and the world's interests are one in the same."[8]

Q #11: How patriotic has Senator Kerry been in honoring and following principles of international law?

- ❑ **4) Very Patriotic**
- ❑ **3) Somewhat Patriotic**
- ❑ **2) Neutral**
- ❑ **1) Somewhat Unpatriotic**
- ❑ **0) Very Unpatriotic**

---

[7] Duncan Campbell, "An Exquisite Danger," *The Guardian/United Kingdom,* June 2, 2004

[8] John Kerry, *A Call to Service,* New York: Viking, 2003, p. 19-20.

Treaties

If America is going to play its part to make the world safe for democracy, it must be a leader not only in military strength and economic vitality, but in its example.

> ***"I have concluded that the ABM treaty hinders our government's ways to protect our people from future terrorist or rogue state missile attacks."***
> **~ George W. Bush, December 13, 2001**

> ***"I will be a president who understands, as every president of the last century did, that multilateralism is not weakness, it is strength. We need a president who understands how to reach out to other countries, build alliances. His father [President H. W. Bush] did a brilliant job of it. We need to do the kind of alliance-building that we have done traditionally."***
> **~ Senator John Kerry, Interview on NBC's Meet the Press, April 18, 2004**

A treaty is simply a formal agreement among two or more states or entities. Treaties with other nations can address issues of peace, commerce, special alliances, or some other international relation or problem. They have become the lifeblood of modern international cooperation. Treaties are negotiated, and as in any negotiation, each side will get something of what it needs, but usually not all. However, there is hope that where disagreement remains, future negotiations may occur.

Treaties have shaped American relations with the world since the mid-19th century. As airline transportation, population growth, weapons of mass destruction, global pollution and electronic communications "shrink" the globe and bring nations into closer proximity, cooperation and respect grow increasingly important. Powerful nations can use treaties to temper their power, and lead by example.

One of the most far-reaching and ambitious of our modern treaties has been the Comprehensive Nuclear Test Ban Treaty. Originating in a 1963 treaty among the United States, the Soviet Union and Great Britain, it ended nuclear testing under water, in the atmosphere, and in outer space. It is a good example of the treaty process. No one got everything they wanted. Underground testing was still allowed. There were no on-site inspections. It was however, the first such agreement after 20 years of negotiations. And ultimately, a more comprehensive arrangement was agreed upon, with emerging nuclear powers being invited into the international effort.

The U.S. is the unquestioned world leader in military and economic strength. Despite leadership in every major category of military armament production, President Bush withdrew from the Comprehensive Nuclear Test Ban Treaty so that we could test and develop even more powerful, “smart” nuclear weapons. President Bush also withdrew from the Anti-Ballistic Missile (ABM) treaty. Even more disturbing to supporters of democratic internationalism, we have developed legal opinions that disregard the accords of the Geneva Conventions regulating the conduct of war and treatment of prisoners since before World War II. Senator John McCain put it bluntly, “Europe would feel better about us if we didn’t keep trashing international treaties.”[9] The importance of participation in such international treaties is underscored by reactions from Russia and China. Russian President Vladimir Putin warned that if the United States pulls out of the ABM treaty, Russia will consider all other arms-control agreements with the United States to be void. China also threatened to beef-up its nuclear arsenal if the United States goes ahead in abandoning the ABM treaty.[10]

If America is going to play its part to make the world safe for democracy, it must be a leader not only in military strength and economic vitality, but in its example. Participation in the world’s treaty efforts is one way to show we are good global citizens. But in times of terrorism and increased national security risks, our patriotic responsibilities are undergoing a long overdue review. Still, it may be in treaties that our national interests are best articulated in our interconnected world.

---

[9] Dick Polman, *The Buffalo News*, April 15, 2004.

[10] Helen Thomas, “Bush Wants to Dump Treaties”, July, 20, 2001, http://www.commondreams.org/views.

Q: Is the United States' current policy on treaties patriotic?

President Bush's Record

National Security advisor Condoleza Rice, speaking for the Bush Administration, said, "The United States and Russia have developed a new relationship where treaties would not have to be negotiated on every warhead and every element of our relationship. I'm saying it's not necessary...to formalize an understanding. President Bush has no intention of reviving the Comprehensive Test Ban Treaty."[11]

In other treaty negotiations, the Bush administration successfully pursued an agreement with Libya's Moammar Gaddafi to surrender his unconventional weapons. And Iran signed an agreement allowing surprise inspection of its nuclear facilities.[12] However, the Bush administration refused to sign an international treaty that would make land mines illegal, opting instead for a ban only on those mines that are not self-destructing.[13]

President Bush has also reacted negatively to other international treaty agreements. He rejected the

Senator Kerry's Record

Senator Kerry has said that American power comes from respect as well as weapons, and that alliances and treaties with other countries matter.[14]

Senator Kerry wrote, "There are times when America must challenge the UN, NATO, and our allies to stand up for their own preferred values. And. . .there are times when America must be challenged to live up to its values as well. America has taken a rare step in human history in arguing that its interests and the world's are one."[15]

Kerry recently proposed an amendment to a nuclear arms reduction agreement requiring annual monitoring reports. In contrast to the Bush Administration, Kerry has argued that now is the time for a determined, all-out effort to secure the world's nuclear materials and weapons of mass destruction. From Kerry's perspective, the only viable solution is a multilateral framework to implement a plan based on the global consensus. He claims that weapons of mass destruction in the control of terrorists represent

---

[11] Ibid.

[12] Dana Milbank, *The Washington Post*, Dec 21, 2003, p. A26.

[13] John Kerry, *Milwaukee Journal Sentinel*, February 13, 2004.

[14] John Kerry, Speech on Iraq and foreign policy, Seattle WA, May 27, 2000.

[15] John Kerry, *A Call to Service,* New York: Viking, 2003, p.19-20.

Bush's Record

International Criminal Court negotiated by United Nations member nations in 1998 that would have jurisdiction over the prosecution of war crimes.

President Bush also rejected the Kyoto climate change treaty, which calls for 38 industrialized countries to reduce greenhouse gas emissions that a majority of scientists worry are contributing to global warming.[16]

Kerry's Record

the most serious threat to international security today. It warrants urgent and global response."[17]

"U.S. rejection of the ABM Treaty would undermine the credibility of U.S. leadership on non proliferation," said Senator Kerry on the floor of the U.S. Senate. "The ABM Treaty can be amended to reflect our changed security environment," he added, "but to abandon it all-together is to welcome an arms race that will make us more vulnerable, not less."[18]

Along with many fellow Democrats, Kerry promises to renegotiate the Kyoto treaty and work toward a global initiative to reduce emissions that contribute to global warming.[19]

---

[16] John Kerry, *Milwaukee Journal Sentinel*, February 13, 2004.

[17] John Kerry, "Interview on NBC's *Meet the Press*", April 18, 2004.

[18] John F. Kerry, Statement on the Floor of the U.S. Senate, Regarding U.S. Missile Defense, May 2, 2001.

[19] John Kerry, *Milwaukee Journal Sentinel*, February 13, 2004.

Bush's Record

Q #12: How patriotic has President Bush been with his approach to international treaties?

- ❑ 4) Very Patriotic
- ❑ 3) Somewhat Patriotic
- ❑ 2) Neutral
- ❑ 1) Somewhat Unpatriotic
- ❑ 0) Very Unpatriotic

Kerry's Record

Q #12: How patriotic has Senator Kerry been with his approach to international treaties?

- ❑ 4) Very Patriotic
- ❑ 3) Somewhat Patriotic
- ❑ 2) Neutral
- ❑ 1) Somewhat Unpatriotic
- ❑ 0) Very Unpatriotic

Cooperation Between Nations

Will the values shaping the way we will deal with the rest of the world be based upon our current might or our historical understanding of right?

> ***"America's foreign policy should respect and nurture our traditional alliances throughout the world and strengthen relations with countries in our own neighborhood."***
> **~ George W. Bush, A Charge to Keep, p. 240, 1999.**

> ***"America has taken a rare step in human history in arguing that its interests and the world's are one."***
> **~ John Kerry, A Call to Service, p.19-20**

For the first 125 years of American history, America was largely an isolationist in foreign policy. We sought distance from European wars and we asked foreign powers to stay out of the Western hemisphere. Through caution about entangling alliances that characterized European affairs, America grew and became strong morally and economically. Today we are the world's most powerful nation and have assumed a role in which we serve as the world's policeman and arbiter for a variety of international issues. In the process, growing numbers of Americans fear we have shifted our historical basis of strength from moral and patriotic values to the values of the dollar and the sword. Others feel that America's current foreign policy is a much needed adjustment that recognizes a scary new world in which terrorists have changed all the rules when it comes to cooperating with other nations.

Regardless of which view resonates with you, shifts in U.S. foreign policy are the result of a more consciously interdependent world. The era of nuclear energy, electronic communications, space travel, modern weaponry, better education, and urbanized society, have each placed new demands on America, as well as on the citizens of every other nation. Travel and immigration have caused us to live in a new and more pluralistic world. These forces of modernity have changed our country and contributed to a shift in our national attitudes and international priorities. As new policies are developed to address these issues, the question foreign policy makers face is this: Will the values shaping the way we will deal with the rest of the world be based upon our current might or our historical understanding of right?

Once again, our nation approaches a crossroads where our foreign policy makers must blend distinctly different strategies in their attempt to foster peace in the world. As Christians, we may ask if the candidate we elect emphasizes the values of the "Prince of Peace," who teaches that peace, and reconcilliation is the way. Or, will he lead with military strength to enforce a peace through conquest and strength of arms?

An alternative may be a third way, the path of a multi-lateral cooperation within the community of nations. How we deal with neighbor nations is an important patriotic concern. Whether we relate through the sword, the dove, or diplomacy, is a vital decision. It must be determined by our patriotic response as citizens who hold the freedom and responsibility to vote.

Q: Should America safeguard its security by maximizing its freedom to act unilaterally or by stressing multilateral collaboration?

President Bush's Record

President Bush has said many times, "We'll go it alone. We cannot entrust the security of the United States to other nations."[20]

Even prior to 9/11 Bush affirmed, "I will have a foreign policy with a touch of iron driven by American interests and American values. A dangerous world requires a sharpened sword . . . I will move quickly to defend our country and allies against blackmail by building missile defense systems."[21]

President Bush believes the U.S. needs to keep a presence in NATO. But the use of the U.S. military needs

Senator Kerry's Record

Senator Kerry has served for 18 years on the Senate Foreign Relations Committee where he has distinguished himself as one of our nation's most consistent voices in favor of international cooperation.

A review of his voting record reveals that Senator Kerry voted for enlarging North Atlantic Treaty Organization (NATO) to include Eastern Europe (H.R. 3167); He also voted for the Gerald B. H. Solomon Freedom Consolidation Act of 2001, a measure that endorsed a further enlargement of the NATO Alliance.[22] Kerry also voted again to pass legislation that would support NATO

[20] George W. Bush said this in various venues, in the face of allied opposition to the proposed attack on Saddam Hussein.

[21] George W. Bush, "Dangerous World", television advertisement, November 18, 1999.

[22] John Kerry on Foreign Policy, On The Issues, 2004.

Bush's Record

in NATO missions must be in the vital interest of the U.S.. President Bush has demanded that if the UN asks for U.S. participation, the UN mission needs to be clear and the exit strategy obvious.[23]

President Bush has also argued that he would reform the United Nations and the International Monetary Fund, and strengthen NATO. Bush supports payment of dues by the U.S. to the United Nations only if its bureaucracy is reformed and America's disproportionate share of its costs is reduced. He would press for reform at international financial institutions such as the International Monetary Fund and the World Bank, including greater transparency and accountability at these institutions themselves. And he would work to strengthen NATO and America's other alliances through greater consultation and sustained American leadership.[24]

But President Bush has also said he would never allow U.S. troops to come under United Nations' command. From President Bush's perspective, "...the UN is an opportunity for people to vent. I say that not facetiously."[25]

Kerry's Record

expansion and authorize military assistance to several eastern European countries and lift assistance restrictions on Slovakia.[26]

Senator Kerry voted to kill a bill imposing trade sanctions on China if it sold weapons and he voted to table an amendment that would require sanctions against China or other countries if they were found to be selling illicit weapons of mass destruction.[27] A Vietnam Veteran, Kerry also voted for ending the Vietnam embargo.[28]

Senator Kerry played a key role in crafting the American response to the events of 9/11, and he has since been a leading Democratic voice on developments in Iraq and Afghanistan, the fight against terrorism, and the Middle East peace process.

[23] George W. Bush, Presidential Debate, Wake Forest University, October 11, 2000.

[24] GeorgeWBush.com: Issues: Policy Points Overview, April 2, 2000.

[26] Mike Allen, *Washington Post*, October 1, 2000, p. A8.

[25] Bill HR. 3167 ; vote number 2002-116 on May 17, 2002

[27] Bill HR. 4444 ; vote number 2000-242 on September 13, 2000

[28] Amendment Agreed to: Yes 62 votes; No 38 votes; Reference: Foreign Relations. Authorization Act FY 94 & 95; Bill S. 1281; vote number 1994-5 on January 27, 1994.

Bush's Record

Q #13: How patriotic has President Bush been regarding international cooperation?

- ❑ 4) Very Patriotic
- ❑ 3) Somewhat Patriotic
- ❑ 2) Neutral
- ❑ 1) Somewhat Unpatriotic
- ❑ 0) Very Unpatriotic

Kerry's Record

Q #13: How patriotic has Senator Kerry been regarding international cooperation?

- ❑ 4) Very Patriotic
- ❑ 3) Somewhat Patriotic
- ❑ 2) Neutral
- ❑ 1) Somewhat Unpatriotic
- ❑ 0) Very Unpatriotic

Peace in Palestine-Israel

America has supported Israel with billions of our tax dollars to maintain the occupation, thereby maintaining the conflict.

"For the sake of peace, this country is committed to helping the Palestinian people establish a democratic and viable state of their own. Israel needs a truly responsible partner in achieving peace. The Palestinian people deserve democratic institutions and responsible leaders. Progress toward this vision creates responsibilities for Israel, the Palestinian people, and Arab nations. All parties must renounce violence and fight terror. Security is the foundation for peace. All parties must embrace democracy and reform and take the necessary steps for peace."
~ George W. Bush, Arab American Institute Presidential Guide.

"My promise to the people of Israel is this: I will never force Israel to make concessions that cost or compromise any of Israel's security . . . We will also never expect Israel to negotiate peace without a credible partner. And it is up to the United States, in my judgment, to do a better job of helping the Arab world to help that partner evolve and to develop."
~ John Kerry, Arab American Institute Presidential Guide.

Peace in Palestine-Israel is a very complicated patriotic issue with no easy solution. However, almost all organizations working for peace (International, Israeli, and Palestinian) in the region agree that the main causes of the conflict are over land. Thus the issues of violence, terrorism, and religious/ethnic tension are not the main causes of the conflict, but rather the symptoms of an unjust solution to division of the land.

When Israel became a state in 1948, it created 750,000 homeless, Palestinian refugees. In 1967 War, Israel occupied the rest of Palestine, leaving Palestinians in an apartheid colonial occupation.

American values of democracy, life, liberty, and the pursuit of happiness may warrant a more evenhanded response to this conflict. Yet historically, America has supported Israel with billions of our tax dollars to maintain the occupation, thereby maintaining the conflict. Israel is the only real democracy in the Middle East, which should be supported, but that democracy is not bestowed upon the Palestinians living in the occupied territories. So only when both Israelis and Palestinians have the freedom, rights, and security to pursue life, liberty, and happiness, will the conflict end.

Christian points of view vary on the matter. Some American Fundamentalists, called Christian Zionists, see the Land as inherently given by God to the Jews, and only when all the Jews return to the Land can the second coming of Christ happen. Ironically their support of Jews stops there, as they are supposed to convert to Christianity or be killed in Armageddon. Other Christians understand that Palestinians and Jews share a Semitic history as well as a common land before Christianity and Islam were born. These Christians relate the current Israeli occupation of Palestine to the Roman occupation during the time of Jesus.

Similarly, there are some Christians and Jews who understand the Biblical promise of Land to the Jews to be dependent on their adherence to God's laws of Justice. So rather than support Israel unconditionally as some Christians do, there are many more verses in the Bible that urge us to do justice (Micah 6:8), love our neighbors (Mark 12:31), and even love our enemies (Luke 6:27). A Christian's options include supportive efforts toward justice for both Palestinians and Israelis, working nonviolently for peace, and being equally critical of their violence toward each other.

Every Administration since the occupation began in 1967 has officially opposed the continual confiscation of land and the building of settlements by the Israeli government as either illegal according to International law, and/or problematic to the Peace Process. But no U.S. Administration has been willing to go beyond words to stop it, because of our strategic and economic relationship with Israel.

Q: Can the U.S. be an evenhanded broker in the Middle East Peace process?

President Bush's Record

President Bush has continued with the status quo: "Israeli settlement activity in occupied territories must stop, and the occupation must end through withdrawal to secure and recognized boundaries, consistent with United

Senator Kerry's Record

Kerry's voting history, like much of Congress, is unabashedly pro-Israel. Although Kerry has criticized President Bush's foreign policy, Kerry's critiques fall short of criticizing Bush's stance on Israel-Palestine. Kerry has

Bush's Record

Nations Resolutions 242 and 338."[29] Like his predecessors, President Bush's Road Map to Peace has been largely lip service and little action.

President Bush echoes the pro-Israel view: "We're going to correct the imbalances of the previous administration on the Mideast conflict. We're going to tilt back toward Israel." Bush continued, "If the two sides don't want peace, there is no way we can force them." And, Colin Powell said, "a pull back by the U.S. would unleash Sharon and the Israeli army." President Bush has added, "Sometimes a show of strength by one side can really clarify things."[30]

President Bush may have created even more roadblocks to peace when he wholeheartedly supported Israel Prime Minister Sharon's disengagement plan.[31] Though Sharon's plan calls for withdrawal from Gaza, it still contradicts Bush's own Road Map by saying that Israel keeps major settlements and a Wall in the West Bank that make it impossible to have a viable Palestinian State. It also dismisses any hope for Palestinian Refugees' Right of Return. This is a major departure from Bush's own previous stance and all the Presidents before him, creating even more anger in the Arab/Muslim world.

Kerry's Record

expressed different views of the Wall, which annexes more of the occupied territories into Israel. "Israel's security fence is a legitimate act of self-defense," Kerry said, a salve to Jews who had been concerned after Kerry described the fence to an Arab American audience in the fall as a "barrier to peace."[32]

To an Arab audience, Senator Kerry stated, "Israel's security will be best assured over the long term if real and lasting peace can be brought to the Middle East. I know that the majority of the Israeli people understand and expect that one day there will be a Palestinian state. Their frustration is that they do not see a committed partner in peace on the Palestinian side. The United States must mediate a series of confidence-building steps which start down the road to peace. Both parties must walk this path together - simultaneously. And the world can help them do it."[33]

Kerry is likely to continue the same stance of non-action and continued financial support of Israel's military occupation if he becomes President.

---

[29] President Bush, Rose Garden Address, Washington, DC, April 4, 2002.

[30] Ron Suskind, *The Price of Loyalty*, New York: Simon & Schuster, 2004, p. 71-72.

[31] George W. Bush, Press Conference, Washington, DC, April 14, 2004.

[32] Ron Kampeas, *Jewish Journal of Greater Los Angeles*, March 5, 2004.

[33] http:aaiusa.org/kerry.htm.

Bush's Record

Q #14: How patriotic has President Bush been in his approach to support for Peace in the Holy Land?

- ❑ 4) Very Patriotic
- ❑ 3) Somewhat Patriotic
- ❑ 2) Neutral
- ❑ 1) Somewhat Unpatriotic
- ❑ 0) Very Unpatriotic

Kerry's Record

Q #14: How patriotic has Senator Kerry been in his approach to support for Peace in the Holy Land?

- ❑ 4) Very Patriotic
- ❑ 3) Somewhat Patriotic
- ❑ 2) Neutral
- ❑ 1) Somewhat Unpatriotic
- ❑ 0) Very Unpatriotic

Global Climate Change

> *"We will require all power plants to meet clean air standards in order to reduce emissions of sulfur dioxide, nitrogen oxide, mercury and carbon dioxide."*
> ~ George Bush campaign speech, Michigan, September 29, 2000

> *"New and potentially catastrophic problems like global climate change call for bold and novel actions. Instead of rising to meet this challenge of defending our national heritage of air, water and land from polluters, however, the president and his appointees have all too often unconditionally surrendered to the demands of polluters."*
> ~ John Kerry, A Call To Service, p. 152.

The scientific debate over global climate change appears to finally have settled. A vast majority of scientists claim there is enough evidence to prove that human activities, such as the burning of oil, coal and natural gas, have induced a discernible rise in average global temperatures over the past 100 years. Though there is a possibility these scientists could be wrong, most governments around the world, particularly in Europe, are making investments based on the presumption that warming trends will continue throughout the 21st century. Even global oil companies, like British Petroleum, are implementing company-wide programs to reduce carbon dioxide (CO2) emissions and investing in alternatives such as solar and wind power.

Of the many environmental issues confronting our earth, this one is genuinely an international concern requiring a foreign policy response. The Kyoto Treaty offered one approach to dealing cooperatively and internationally with an environmental concern that touches all nations of the world.

According to estimates by the United Nations, the U.S. is responsible for more than a quarter of the world's CO2 emissions. Because the population of the U.S. is only 4% of the global total, it is clear that the U.S. must play a major role in reducing global CO2 emissions in order to stabilize our atmosphere.[34]

While sources of CO2 emissions are spread throughout the economy, ranging from agriculture to everyday household activities, the single largest source is the burning of fossil fuels. Americans love affair with the automobile is a critical

[34] "Global Warming 101", Natural Resources Defense Council (www.nrdc.org), January 21, 2003.

contributor to the climate change conundrum. Yet the energy industry that lights up our homes and keeps us cool and warm is equally to blame.

The recent Pentagon report, "An Abrupt Climate Change Scenario and Its Implications for United States National Security," finds that temperatures could rise or fall 4–6° F in a single decade. The report points out that wars could break out over access to water, food and energy, creating millions of refugees.

With this new information, it becomes critical that international governments can agree on fundamental shifts in business-as-usual activities.

The Christian community, in particular, strives to live in the presence of the holy within creation. They feel they have a call to holiness; a duty to avoid those things that contaminate our own health and the well-being of the earth.

Q: Is it patriotic for the U.S. to develop its own unique approach to addressing global climate change?

President Bush's Record

During the 2000 presidential campaign, candidate Bush pledged to require reductions in private sector emissions contributing to global climate change. This position by President Bush surprised business lobbyists as well as environmentalists. Bush changed his position, however, once elected to the White House.[35]

President Bush flatly rejected the Kyoto climate treaty negotiated in Japan in 1997, which called for 38 industrialized nations around the world to make steep cuts in CO2 and other global warming gases.[36] (Former

Senator Kerry's Record

Senator Kerry has sat in on international negotiations over global climate change for more than a decade. In 1992, he helped draft the Framework Convention on Climate Change at the 1992 Earth Summit in Rio, Brazil. He served in the congressional delegation to the 1997 Kyoto sessions and year 2000 The Hague, Netherlands climate change talks.[37]

During Bush's term in office, Kerry introduced legislation to hasten up the process for the U.S. to develop a comprehensive global climate change mitigation

[35] "Clear Skies Initiative," EPA Press Release, February 22, 2003 (http://www.epa.gov/air/clearskies/prerels.html).

[36] Dick Thompason, "Why US Environmentalists Pin Hopes On Europe," *Time Magazine*, March 26, 2001.

[37] John Kerry For President, Environment and Energy Policy, www.johnkerry.com.

Bush's Record

President Clinton approved Kyoto, but he was never able to muster approval in the U.S. Congress.) Bush has maintained that more study was required before America should agree to mandatory changes in the business practices of U.S. businesses and lifestyle choices of citizens.

In February 2003, the Bush administration revealed a new voluntary reduction program that would reduce CO2 "emission intensity" by 18% by 2012.[38] (Emission intensity is defined as CO2 pollution relative to economic output.) Bush administration figures show, nevertheless, that overall releases of CO2 will by 2012 actually increase by 14% due to population growth.[39] This 14% growth rate is identical to CO2 growth rates experienced during the previous decade.

The Bush Administration has not only fought international efforts to respond to global climate change, but has also weighed in on state efforts. The Bush Administration joined U.S. automakers in filing a lawsuit opposing a recent California law that requires CO2 emission reductions in all vehicles sold in California beginning in 2009.

Kerry's Record

program. Kerry also successfully attached to the 2001 Bush Administration budget amendments to "reduce greenhouse gas emissions, address global climate change concerns, protect the global environment, promote domestic energy security and to provide funding for voluntary programs that will reduce greenhouse gas emissions."[40]

If elected president, Kerry will craft a new binding treaty with the rest of the nations that signed Kyoto. It is Kerry's hope that a fresh approach could "take us beyond Kyoto to protect the global environment."[41]

Kerry's proposed domestic strategy to address global climate change includes [a renewable energy trust with a] national target of producing 20% of the nation's energy from renewable fuels by 2020. If this goal is met, it will offset the need to import 2 million barrels of oil daily and create 500,000 jobs here in the U.S.[42]

---

[38] "Bush Administration Launches 'Climate VISION'," Department of Energy Press Release, February 12, 2003.

[39] Analysis of Bush Administration Greenhouse Target, World Resources Institute, revised February 12, 2003.

[40] Rick Heffern, "Activists Battle Bush Assault on California Green Laws," *National Catholic Reporter*, March 14, 2003.

[41] League of Conservation Voters Presidential Questionnaire, August 8, 2003.

[42] www.JohnKerry.com/issues/energy/index.html, p. 1.

Bush's Record

Q #15: How patriotic has President Bush been in his efforts to address global climate change?

- ❑ 4) Very Patriotic
- ❑ 3) Somewhat Patriotic
- ❑ 2) Neutral
- ❑ 1) Somewhat Unpatriotic
- ❑ 0) Very Unpatriotic

Kerry's Record

Q #15: How patriotic has Senator Kerry been in his efforts to address global climate change?

- ❑ 4) Very Patriotic
- ❑ 3) Somewhat Patriotic
- ❑ 2) Neutral
- ❑ 1) Somewhat Unpatriotic
- ❑ 0) Very Unpatriotic

CHAPTER 4

Education

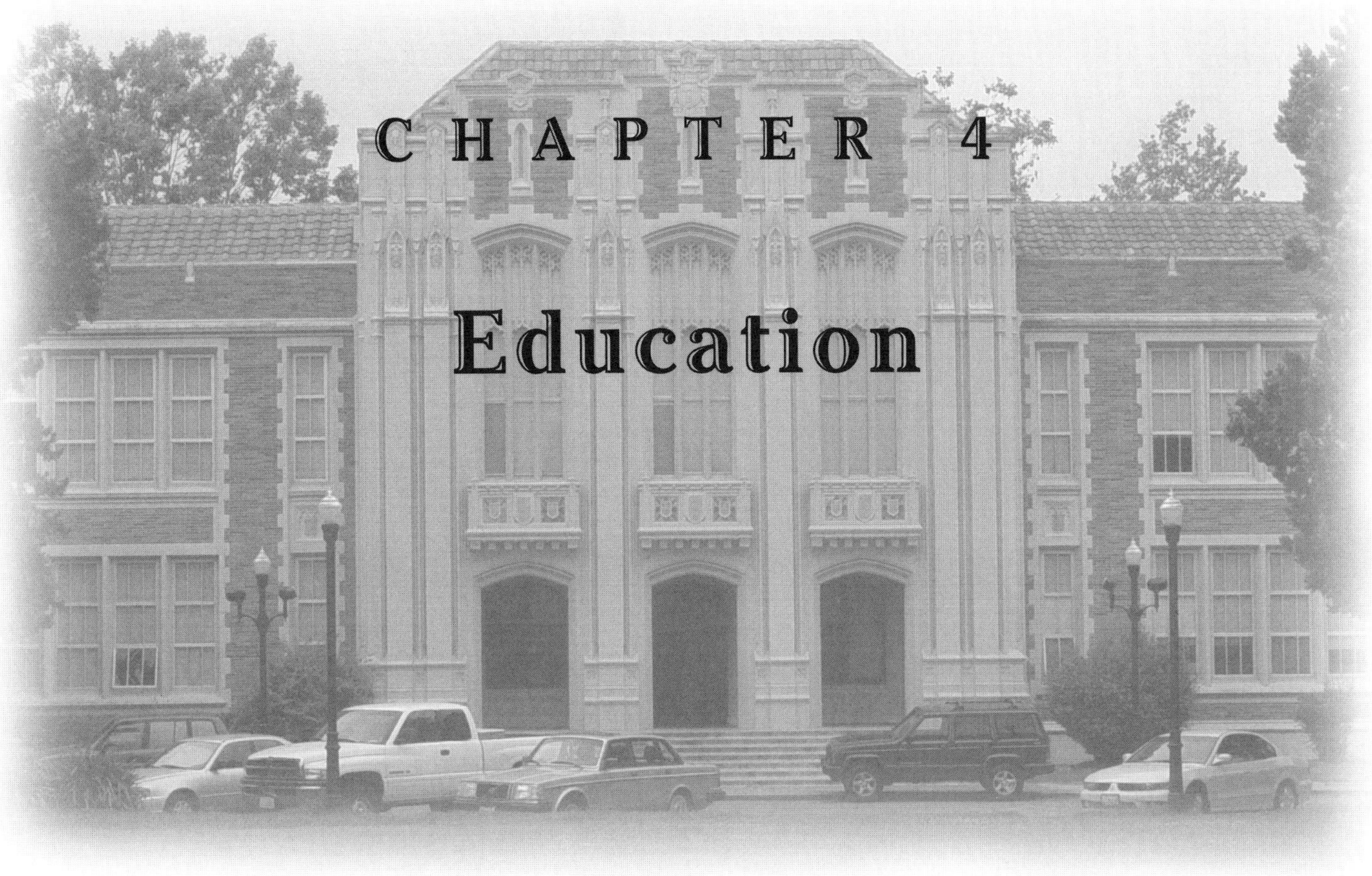

INTRODUCTION

"Whenever the people are well-informed, they can be trusted with their own government." - Thomas Jefferson

Universal public education is the bedrock of American patriotism. A healthy democracy needs an educated, informed populace. Participation in our democracy is what makes our representative government work. Fulfilling our civic responsibility means speaking honestly and openly about critical issues. People fully participate in democracy when they understand the issues and have a good education to back them up.

Perhaps no issue is more prone to a good patriotic debate than how education is accomplished in our country. If patriotism is love of country and concern for the best interests of all its citizens, how then is education best achieved?

Thomas Jefferson set forth the ideal. He envisioned a system of tax supported free schools for all. Today, U.S. grade schools and high schools are still free. School is also compulsory until you are sixteen years old.

Our public education system is focused on children. They deserve the best opportunity to live a full and meaningful life. Every child should have the opportunity to grow and develop his or her own potential. Public schools should build community, recognize our common humanity, and eliminate social inequality. These are, of course, lofty goals and ideals.

Current President George W. Bush has summed up the challenge facing America today in the following way: "I worry that we're being divided into two nations, separate and unequal: one nation with the tools and confidence to seek the American dream; another nation that is being left behind. We risk becoming two societies: one that reads, and one that can't, one that dreams and one that doesn't. We are united by a common bond of history and citizenship. President Lincoln reminded us that America is not just a collection of states or individuals. We are a single, moral community, with obligations to one another. We are America."[2]

Senator John Kerry has this to say about government's role in fostering an educated society: "Education is as basic to America's future as any you can imagine . . . The longstanding American aspirations of equal opportunity and upward mobility depend on an educational system that equips our people- all of our people . . . Maintaining the commitment to keep public schools public- in the broad sense of ensuring that they provide an equal foundation of knowledge and skills to every single child- is a hard but essential struggle. The common investment we make in public education is a big part of what makes our country a commonwealth in which we can share in the fruits of a wise investment."[3]

The ideals our elected officials put forward have deep roots in our Judeo-Christian heritage. Of course, two thousand years ago there was no such thing as public education. Public education is a creation of our modern democratic culture. Our biblical ancestors were interested in wisdom. They read scripture and debated its meaning. Many of us know the story of Jesus arguing with the priests in the Temple. Rabbi in Hebrew means "teacher." Like the Greeks who gathered around their philosophers to learn, the Disciples gathered around Jesus to hear his word and follow his way.

The value of being educated is reflected in the beginning of the Book of Proverbs:

For learning (is) about wisdom and instruction, for understanding words of insight, for gaining instruction in wise dealing, righteousness, justice and equity; to teach shrewdness to the simple, knowledge and prudence to the young- let the wise also hear and gain in learning, and the discerning acquire skill, to understand the proverb and the figure, the words of the wise and their riddles.[4]

This passage from the Bible sets a high standard regarding an ideal education. In practice, we face a long list of wants and needs when it comes to education. Most parents see school as a way for their children to learn good citizenship and important skills. They want education to open the door to more job opportunities than they may have had.

Parents also want help with the character education of their children. It begins at home, and in religious communities, but they want schools to support them,

[2] George W. Bush, *A Charge to Keep* (New York: Morrow, 1999), p.228.
[3] John Kerry, *A Call to Service* (New York:Viking Penguin, 2003), p.228.
[4] Proverbs 1:2-6. (New Revised Standard Version, The New Oxford Bible with the Apocrypha).

too. The universal ethical values we try to teach our children, such as respect, honesty, fairness, responsibility, compassion, gratitude, friendship, peace, and self-discipline, need reinforcement in our culture.

Government gains legitimacy with its citizens by providing a good education. People feel better paying taxes if they know that their children and grand children are receiving a quality education. American business benefits, too. An educated workforce is highly sought after in today's very competitive, global economy.

High quality, reasonably priced public education is needed now more than ever. For the true patriot, life, liberty and pursuit of happiness are directed toward all people as a community and not just toward the selfish desires of one individual, one economic or social class, one gender, race or ethnic group, or any particular ideology.

Woodrow Wilson said, "Nations are renewed from the bottom, not from the top."[5] A functioning democracy requires participation from educated, informed citizens. Electing politicians that make public education their priority, will make this nation a stronger republic.

"Enlighten the people, generally, and tyranny and opressions of body and mind will vanish like spirits at the dawn of day."
~ Thomas Jefferson, letter to Dupont de Nemours, April 24, 1816

[5] Diane Ravitch, Ed., *The American Reader* (New York: Harper Collins, 1990), p. 224.

Federal Financial Support For Public Education

"We are a nation where a majority of fourth graders in our cities can't read or understand simple children's books; a nation whose ninth graders too often have fourth grade reading skills, and where the achievement gap between rich and poor, Anglo and minority, is wide."
~ George W. Bush, A Charge To Keep, p. 232.

"The roles of federal, state, and local governments in education vary enormously throughout the country. In particular, the reliance on property taxes to fund public education has resulted in large inequities in the resources available for schools."
~ John Kerry, A Call To Service, p. 99.

America once had the best public education system in the world. It was primarily the responsibility of state government and individual school districts. If you had a child in the public education system, you probably knew a school teacher. He or she might have been a relative or neighbor. You trusted them to provide a quality education to your children.

Those teachers taught much the same way as teachers do today. Students attend classes with 20-30 students. They listen to lectures, do lab experiments, carry on discussions, write papers, and take tests. Teachers still assign homework and expect good behavior. Though now funded from outside sources, teachers and schools still support the extra curricular activities that help students become creative, well-rounded adults.

Inequalities exist now as they did then. Discrimination in our school systems is often based on the wealth of the local community or ethnic and racial differences. The importance of public education has increased over time, fueling the need for more formal education, while still maintaining a focus on the "equality-for-all" ideal.

American public education serves a large number of people. In 1900, only 10% of American adolescents aged 14 to 17 were enrolled in high school. Just over a century later, 86% of students graduated from high school in 2002.

Except in the inner cities, public school facilities improved for most students in the 20th century. More money was spent on education, resulting in better teachers' salaries, and improvements in curricula. Special educational needs also received attention for the first time. Spending on students in public elementary and secondary schools increased from $2,101 per pupil in the 1959-1960 academic year (in constant 1998-1999 dollars) to $7,013 per pupil in the 1998-1999 academic year.[6]

Today, public schools are funded by a combination of property taxes and state and federal funding, with increasing percentages of funding now coming from the federal government. Schools that are in low-income neighborhoods generally have less money to pay teachers and to provide school supplies. These schools also often are required to offer tutoring and other services needed by disadvantaged students. If we would like all of our citizens to have a good education in order to participate in our democracy, some schools will need more help than others. It's the patriotic thing to do. That is one of the key goals of the Bush Administration program known as "No Child Left Behind."

The No Child Left Behind Act of 2001 had broad bipartisan support. In exchange for "accountability for results," states and school districts would receive funding, resources and the flexibility to get the job done right. Support was to be there for students and for the public schools to fund the needed education improvements.

No Child Left Behind was designed to help parents as well as our country in general. Among many of the laudable goals of the program were its support for the following: Early Learning programs; the measuring of student performance; providing new information to parents; giving failing schools greater options; and ensuring more resources for schools.[7]

Enacting the law was a step toward greater support for public education. Fully funding the effort has been the larger challenge.

---

[6] "Public Education in the United States", *Microsoft ® Online Encyclopedia*, 2004. http://encarta.msn.com(c)1997-2004MicrosoftCorporation.

[7] "Education Issues Brief," Bush/Cheney'04, 2004 http://www.georgewbush.com/Education/Brief.aspx.

Q: Is it patriotic to give all public schools throughout the country the same amount of federal financial support?

President Bush's Record

President Bush's major educational program, the No Child Left Behind Act, was passed by Congress. In order to meet its goals, Congress authorized a $5.6 billion increase in title 1 in spending for low-income children. President Bush budgeted only one billion dollars for Title one. By cutting funding by more than 80%, the congressional research service estimates President Bush's No Child Left Behind program budget does not include almost 12 million children or 16% of the children in America.[8]

In the No Child Left Behind Act, Congress authorized an expansion of transportation and other support services to an additional 130,000 homeless children. President Bush's budget does not provide any current funding for this program. No Child Left Behind also authorized increased funding to help school districts meet the new government mandate that all teachers in core academic subjects be highly qualified by the end of the 2005 through 2006. President Bush's budget trains 92,000 fewer teachers than were promised by the Act, which in turn affects the lives of about 10 million children. [9]

Senator Kerry's Record

Senator Kerry voted for The No Child Left Behind Act. But Kerry still advocates the full funding for initiatives included in the Act. John Kerry's education plan calls for greater accountability in schools and he is a longtime supporter of the so-called "accountability in education" movement.[10]

John Kerry is sponsoring a "National Education Trust Fund" to make sure that, for the first time in U.S. history, the federal government meets its obligation to fully fund our educational priorities and make sure that schools meet high standards.[11]

In 2001, Senator Kerry voted for Bill S1, which encouraged funding of smaller classes instead of private tutors by assisting state and local education agencies in recruiting additional teachers. Kerry also voted 'yes' on spending $448 billion of the federal income tax cut in 2001 on education and debt reduction, reducing the size of the $1.6 trillion tax cut, and increasing national education spending by $250 billion (and an additional debt reduction increase of $244 billion.) Senator Kerry

[8] "No Child Left Behind legislation Report," Congressional Research Services. http://www.ncseonline.org/nlc/crsreports/legislative/leg-3.pdf.
[9] "George W. Bush on Education," On The Issues, 2004. http://www.issues2000.org/2004/George_W_Bush_Education.html.
[10] "Kerry Supports No Child Left Behind," *Washington Post*, May 9, 2004.
[11] "National Education Trust Fund," John Kerry President, 2004. Http://www.johnkerry.com/issues/education.html.

Bush's Record

Bush encouraged allocating public money to private primary and secondary education by expanding deductible savings accounts eligibility criteria. Bush also favors earmarking tax dollars for religious schools, and "portable" education funding parents could use to fund their child's education as they please. He is on record in support of public policies allowing vouchers and private charter schools to receive public education dollars.[12]

Q #16: How patriotic is President Bush regarding adequate funding for universal public education?

- ❑ 4) Very Patriotic
- ❑ 3) Somewhat Patriotic
- ❑ 2) Neutral
- ❑ 1) Somewhat Unpatriotic
- ❑ 0) Very Unpatriotic

Kerry's Record

co-sponsored the Public Education Reinvestment, Reinvention, and Responsibility Act (the 3 R's) in 2001. This Act would provide public schools with increased funding and flexibility, help close the achievement gap, and give broad latitude to state and local officials in meeting the standards (including helping immigrant students master English to meet the higher standards). The Act would also improve teacher quality.[13]

Q #16: How patriotic is Senator Kerry regarding adequate funding for universal public education?

- ❑ 4) Very Patriotic
- ❑ 3) Somewhat Patriotic
- ❑ 2) Neutral
- ❑ 1) Somewhat Unpatriotic
- ❑ 0) Very Unpatriotic

[12] "George W. Bush on Education," On The Issues, 2004. http://www.issues2000.org/2004/George_W_Bush_Education.html
[13] "John Kerry on Education," On The Issues, 2004. http://www.issues2000.org/2004/John_Kerry_Education.html

Vouchers

> *"Vouchers are up to the states. If you want to do a voucher program . . . fine . . . I believe in local control of schools."*
> ~ George W. Bush, On The Issues, 2004

> *"I understand why parents want more choices and I believe they should have more choices in public schools. But public schools need resources and support, and vouchers drain them both."*
> ~ John Kerry, On The Issues, 2004

Should we pursue the public good with public education? Or should we work to see that our own children excel and succeed, no matter what happens to other children? These are the real questions behind the debate on vouchers, a word referring to tax-supported financial grants that can be used to pay for education at private schools. We cannot ask the nation's founders what they thought of vouchers, but we can look at how they envisioned public financial support of education.

The founders clearly believed schooling should serve everyone regardless of background and give all an equal chance. It is a patriot's responsibility. This is the egalitarian ideal of the Declaration of Independence, that all are created equal, and endowed with inalienable rights. The attempt to provide for an education for all was evident in the American conscience even before the founding of our Republic.

The first secondary school in the United States that was publicly funded was Boston Latin School, which was founded in 1635. As early as the 17th century, colonial law extracted penalties for communities that failed to provide for public education systems for local children.

Churches were a primary force in establishing public schools in the early days of our nation. Our Founding Fathers believed that education and faithfulness went hand-in-hand. Of course, the root of the commitment to a broad public education was a desire for people to read the Bible and the ancient Classics. These same early church leaders were also patriots who viewed public education as necessary to ensure our democratic freedoms.

Thomas Jefferson proposed a system of free schools for all persons that would be publicly supported through taxes. He wanted education to be separate from religious indoctrination. However, Jefferson's plans for universal education and publicly funded schools did not materialize until the mid-19th century. Until then, most education was a mix of local municipal efforts and private institutions.

What we think of as universal publicly funded education was first established in the 1830s and 1840s. Education visionaries such as Horace Mann and the "Common School" movement inspired them. To these Americans, "common" meant both that all young people were being educated and that education's contents are of equal quality and taught the same way. By the turn of the 20th century, the reformers' work had largely been accomplished. It was clear that the Founding Fathers and our nation's initial education visionaries expected public money to support public schools, not private ones.

Current debates over the U.S. education system is influenced by contrary perspectives: the ideal of universal publicly funded education that serves the public good; and the private desire of parents to pass on to their children an educational advantage and social advancement even at the expense of the common good. The latter desire lurks in the background behind the debate on vouchers, especially when they are used to fund private education and private schools since they leave less tax dollars for improving the public education system upon which most Americans rely.

Q: What would our forefathers think about public financial vouchers for education used to pay for education at private schools?

President Bush's Record

President Bush's "The No Child Left Behind" Act promises an estimated $200 million for charter schools

Senator Kerry's Record

Senator Kerry has been supportive of 'public' school choice and the use of 'public' federal funding. He

Bush's Record

to expand parental choice and frees local school districts to spend up to half their federal education dollars where they believe it will do the most good for their students.[14] President Bush's policies include increasing choices for parents in the education of their children by allowing federal funds to be used for public and private school choice and giving parents of Title I students federal education dollars in a portable account to use in a school or program of their choice.[15]

Responding to critics who dislike vouchers and who support increased funding for public schools, Bush has stated: "If the poorest of the poor remain in trapped schools, that money that would go to the school should go to the parent so the parent gets to make a choice."[16] President Bush said that much of the money earmarked for the struggling schools would be broken apart and distributed to parents in the form of payments –"vouchers" – that may be used to transfer students to private schools.

President Bush has avoided using the politically laden term "vouchers", and instead says federal education money should be "portable." Bush would in effect give vouchers of up to $1,500 each to students. These vouchers would be financed with money drawn from the Title I program.[17]

Kerry's Record

is a sponsor of the Public Education Reinvestment, Reinvention and Responsibility Act, an attempt at developing some common ground between Republicans and Democrats on federal education issues. The legislation proposed investing $35 billion over the next 5 years to target the persistent achievement gap between poor and more affluent students.

Senator Kerry voted 'no' on a motion to invoke cloture on a bill aimed at allowing states to waive certain federal rules normally required in order to use federal school aid. (A 'yes' vote implied support of vouchers.) Senator Kerry voted 'no' on legislation that would have amended the District of Columbia spending measure, imposing what Kerry and critics claimed was an unconstitutional school voucher program on the District of Columbia.[18]

In describing his Educational Trust Fund proposal, Senator Kerry said, "Tell the truth about vouchers - that they weaken public education, make it harder to build good citizens, and hurt those most in need. Vouchers aren't choice; they are a bad choice that would leave even more children behind. They don't reform our schools - they run away from them. My resolve (is to) fight for real change and real resources for our public schools. I have never

[16] "Education Issues Brief," Bush/Cheney '04, 2004.

[15] "Policy Points Overview," Bush/Cheney '04, 2004.

[16] "George W. Bush on Education," On The Issues, 2004.

[17] Ibid.

[18] "John Kerry on Education," On The Issues, 2004.

Bush's Record

Q #17: How patriotic is President Bush when it comes to public vouchers for education used to pay for education at private schools?

- ❑ 4) Very Patriotic
- ❑ 3) Somewhat Patriotic
- ❑ 2) Neutral
- ❑ 1) Somewhat Unpatriotic
- ❑ 0) Very Unpatriotic

Kerry's Record

supported vouchers. I will never support them. And if it ever comes to my desk, I'll veto vouchers or voucher-like programs the day that bill arrives."[19]

Q #17: How patriotic is Senator Kerry when it comes to public vouchers for education used to pay for education at private schools?

- ❑ 4) Very Patriotic
- ❑ 3) Somewhat Patriotic
- ❑ 2) Neutral
- ❑ 1) Somewhat Unpatriotic
- ❑ 0) Very Unpatriotic

[19] "One Hundred Days to Change America," John Kerry President, 2004. Http://www.johnkerry.com/issues/100days/education.html.

Performance Standards

"Accountability is empty without local control ... local parents and teachers care far more about what happens in local schools than distant bureaucrats."
~ George W. Bush, A Charge To Keep, p. 233

"Our goal should be to empower every public school to establish clear expectations and accountability and be allowed much more freedom to innovate in how results are achieved."
~ John Kerry, A Call To Service, p. 108

A label on a child's Superman costume issued this warning: "Wearing of this garment does not enable you to fly." This summarizes the dilemma we face when we talk about performance standards in public education. Having performance standards does not guarantee that learning will happen. There is no simple, objective measurement of school success, no "magic flying cape."

Most parents have set high standards for their children. While we want our children to enjoy school -- pep rallies, sports events, field trips, proms, and all the rest of the social activities that schools offer – we are most concerned that they are receiving a viable education for the 21st century.

The U.S. education system was once the envy of the industrialized world. Times have changed, and so have schools. The 1983 federal report "A Nation at Risk" suggested that American students were out-performed on international academic tests by students from other industrial societies."[20] The response to the report here in the U.S. included more effective and increased assessments of student performance conducted by each state and mandated curriculum requirements. There was also an increase in federal funding and federal control over local schools.

[20] "Public Education in the United States," Microsoft ®) Online Encyclopedia, 2004.

In the early years of the current "accountability movement," education professionals took an expansive view of performance. Your child took uniform tests. He or she also submitted work portfolios and projects. Teachers were able to review and assess each student's academic achievement. There was no 'one-size fits all' mentality, no 'magic flying cape'.

With "The No Child Left Behind Act," accountability shifts primarily to standardized federal tests. This approach appeals to those parents that feel frustrated by poor education and failed schools. The rationale for this new federal approach is partly financial. These standard tests are less expensive, and easier to implement nationwide, than any other testing program. They offer visible, quantitative results. Performance can be evaluated by checking to see if test scores are improving. The question is, are these standard performance tests enough to correct the larger social and political issues of American education?

There are other questions, too. Will states water-down their testing standards to avoid federal sanctions? Will teachers simply teach with an eye toward having students pass a uniform exam? Is that what American public education is all about? One teacher commented: "If I were asked to enumerate ten educational stupidities, the giving of grades would be at the head of the list ... If I can't give a child a better reason for studying than a grade on a report card, I ought to lock up my desk and go home and stay there." [21]

The American public school has always been looked upon as a place in our culture that promotes the patriotic ideal of equality in the midst of diversity. The value of the individual is long celebrated in our culture.

The detailed technical concerns surrounding school performance standards are not easy to understand. Patriotically, we can address the broad questions. We must decide if we want to trust our educators to implement a system that pays attention to our child's individual, educational needs, as opposed to giving ourselves a 'good grade' based on a standard that might not meet the distinct needs of our community.

---

[21] Dorothy DeZouche, quoted from "Educational Quotes". Http://home.att.net/~quotations/education.html

Q: Is it patriotic for the federal government to mandate school performance standards for local schools?

President Bush's Record

President Bush wants to make federal public school funding contingent on each state giving standardized tests in math and reading whose results would be published and available to the general public. When Bush was campaigning for President in 2000, he proposed a $47 million, 10-year plan to improve pupil achievement.

As President, Bush currently supports paying for states to participate in an annual National Assessment in Education Progress sample exam in reading and math.[22] President Bush said in his Budget Message to congress: Children should be tested ... every year. ... Measuring is the only way to know whether all our children are learning."

President Bush, in his 2004 State of the Union address, again said, "testing is the only way to identify and help students who are falling behind. It was testing and not choice that he fought hardest to preserve in passing the No Child Left Behind Act.[23]

Bush claims his Administration has increased funding for education by 36% increase since 2001. Still, President Bush's new federal requirements for student testing impose large costs on state and local governments, both levels of government suffering from their own budget shortfalls.

Senator Kerry's Record

Senator Kerry supported the No Child Left Behind Law because of his long-standing commitment to assuring every U.S. child can meet high performance standards. According to Kerry, his proposed National Educational Trust Fund will guarantee that U.S. public schools get the funding they need and the funding they deserve to meet the federal performance standards. His approach relies more on incentives than on the types of penalties included in the Bush Administration's approach. Kerry has promised to reward, not punish, states that make progress and implement high standards."[24]

Senator Kerry believes it is time to stop sending mandates from Washington to school districts without providing the resources needed to carry them out. In his Democratic 2004 primary debate at the University of Southern California, Senator Kerry said, "...what's happening under the Bush administration is that they are disrespecting teachers, they're making it punitive. The way they're applying the adequate yearly progress standard, that you can have a few kids who enter the school and may have language difficulties that year, and they could drag the whole school into a status of failure. It's so arbitrary

[22] "Policy Points Overview," Bush/Cheney '04, 2004.

[23] "George W. Bush on Education," On The Issues, 2004.

[24] "Speeches," John Kerry President, 2004. Http://www.johnkerry.com/pressroom/speeches/spc_2003_1125.html.

Bush's Record

Bush has yet to push the Republican Congress for the full amounts authorized by the No Child Left Behind Act. GOP senator Olympia Snow of Maine commented last year: "It leaves us open to the charge of unfunded mandates."[25]

A report by the Rand Corporation, a non-partisan think tank, challenges claims by then Governor Bush that education vastly improved under his watch between 1994 and 1998. Although students did much better on state administered tests – giving rise to the idea of a "Texas miracle" in education (a centerpiece of President Bush's presidential campaign) – those improvements were not reflected when students took a national test.[26]

Kerry's Record

that it's destroying morale of the school system. I want standards and accountability. But you cannot do it without the resources, and you also can't do it in a way where you turn schools into testing factories!"[27]

Kerry voted "yes" on national education standards as far back as 1994, when he cast his vote in favor of the Goals 2000: Educate America Act (HR 1804).

[25] "What Bush Left Unsaid in the State of the Union Address," Fact Check, 2004. Http://www.FactCheck.org. (See January, 2004 archives).

[26] "George W. Bush On Education," On The Issues, 2004.

[27] "John Kerry on Education," On The Issues, 2004. Http://www2.acf.dhhs.gov/programs/budget/index.html.

Bush's Record

Q #18: How patriotic about public education is President Bush regarding mandated school performance standards?

- ❑ 4) Very Patriotic
- ❑ 3) Somewhat Patriotic
- ❑ 2) Neutral
- ❑ 1) Somewhat Unpatriotic
- ❑ 0) Very Unpatriotic

Kerry's Record

Q #18: How patriotic about public education is Senator Kerry regarding mandated school performance standards?

- ❑ 4) Very Patriotic
- ❑ 3) Somewhat Patriotic
- ❑ 2) Neutral
- ❑ 1) Somewhat Unpatriotic
- ❑ 0) Very Unpatriotic

Early Childhood Education Programs

> *"Each of our children needs . . . an equal opportunity . . . even before school starts. On the first day of school, children need to know letters and numbers. They need a strong vocabulary. And they need to love books. These are the building blocks of learning, and this nation must provide them."*
> ~ George Bush, "Head Start", Head Start 2004

> *"Each and every child in this country is valuable because they are our future as a society. We cannot afford to lose a single child to ill-health, under education, abuse, addition, jail, or gun violence. America's highest goal should be for every child to grow up to be a successful young adult healthy, educated, free, secure and a good citizen."*
> ~ John Kerry, "Head Start", John Kerry President, 2004

Fostering a young child's learning is a complex task. We begin learning about life the moment we are born and continue the rest of our lives. Early Childhood education is made easier when there is sound parenting, good health care, and a variety of support systems. It often takes the efforts of the whole community to successfully raise children.

Many primitive societies focused on the communal raising of children. Our modern world has chosen to emphasize the family, but we still involve others. For example, many young parents ask grandparents and siblings to "babysit." Most parents today call on an extended family system of neighbors, friends, churches, clubs, and government support programs to help educate our children. However, not all parents have access to all these options. In our modern world with its stresses and demands, some children will be "left behind" unless we fulfill our patriotic responsibility to love our country and show concern for the best interests of all our citizens.

Over the years, the federal government has established a number of programs grounded in a strong commitment to the common good of all the citizens. Though far from perfect, many of these have been valuable additions to the "extended family" that helps raise our children. Head Start is one of these successful government programs. This year marks its 39th anniversary. At this point, funding runs out in 2006.

In 1964, the federal government asked a panel of child development experts to draw up a program to help parents and communities meet the needs of disadvantaged preschool children. From this emerged "Project Head Start," an effort to help break the cycle of poverty by providing preschool children of low-income families with a comprehensive program to meet the emotional, social, health, nutritional, and psychological needs.

The highly successful "Project Head Start" currently serves children and their families throughout the United States, with both long established efforts and fresh innovative early childhood projects. All Project Head Start programs are managed locally to meet the needs of the families involved. The Department of Health and Human Services directly funds 19,000 centers, each operated by community groups, faith-based organizations or local public schools. That is quite an "extended family," serving more than 900,000 three-and four-year olds and their families.[28]

Our young children cannot be inoculated against all the harsh realities of life, particularly the disadvantages of poverty. No government program can successfully make up for what a hard life takes away. As patriots, our commitment to the common good of the nation, its families and their children, helps compensate for the disadvantages. As citizens of this nation, we can provide opportunities to the most disadvantaged among us to learn basic skills early in life. This can place our young children on the path to success. Supporting early childhood education is one way to ensure our students' success and better provide for America's future.

[28] Krista Kafer, *A Head Start for Poor Children?*, The Heritage Foundation, 2004. Http://www.heritage.org/Research/Education/bg1755.cfm

Q: Is remaining committed to early childhood education for the youngest and most vulnerable of our nation's children a worthy patriotic act?

President Bush's Record

In a speech to the 2000 Republican National Convention, President Bush said, "Now is the time to make Head Start an early learning program, teach all our children to read, and renew the promise of America's public schools."

According to the Children's Defense Fund, President Bush's 2005 budget freezes "Head Start" enrollment at 2004 levels. Currently, 40 percent of eligible Head Start children and 97 percent of Early Start eligible toddlers do not receive services.

President Bush's No Child Left Behind advocated improving Project Head Start to make sure that it is an early learning and education program that prepares young children to succeed academically. According to Bush, all Project Head Start programs will be evaluated and renewal contracts will only be given to those who use the curriculum to prepare the children. Those who do not rely upon federal curriculum will be discontinued and the contract will be open to competitive bid.[29]

Bush has been critical of federal education programs in the past. "Much of what the federal government sponsors

Senator Kerry's Record

Senator Kerry has promised to make early childhood education a top national priority. "Our early childhood education system will be a model for the world," Kerry has claimed.[30] He has referred to breakthrough findings in the world of science regarding how critical the early years of life are in shaping every future learning and development opportunity. He has proposed to expand pre-kindergarten education and other similar platforms for cognitive learning. Kerry has sponsored an effort that provides funding for families to increase and coordinate early childhood development initiatives.[31]

John Kerry signed "The Hyde Park Declaration, A New Agenda for the Decade", which also lends support for focusing on universal access to pre-kindergarten education.[32] Senator Kerry has promised he will work to fully fund the Head Start program so that every 3 and 4-year old in poverty can receive the comprehensive cognitive, social/emotional, health, and parent education services needed for success. His website states Kerry "will never block grant Head Start like President Bush has proposed doing, putting at risk an important and

---

[29] *"George W. Bush on Education,"* On The Issues, 2004.

[30] *"Educational Trust Fund,"* John Kerry President, 2004.

[31] John Kerry, *A Call to Service*, New York, NY, Viking, 2003, p.114.

[32] *"John Kerry On Education,"* On The Issues, 2004

Bush's Record

is sloppy and trendy, heralding self-esteem over basic skills," he wrote in his book, *A Charge To Keep*. Governor Bush's early childhood development efforts in Texas relied largely on the work of Laura Bush. Mrs. Bush launched the Family Literacy Initiative for Texas, a statewide effort to complement education and reading reforms. The program received almost a million dollars in grants.[33]

Q #19: How patriotic about public education is President Bush where established and successful educational programs exist, such as Head Start?

- ❑ **4) Very Patriotic**
- ❑ **3) Somewhat Patriotic**
- ❑ **2) Neutral**
- ❑ **1) Somewhat Unpatriotic**
- ❑ **0) Very Unpatriotic**

Kerry's Record

proven successful program. There is no more important investment in our children. We must get our kids off to the right start and give them a shot at meeting their fullest potential."[34]

Q #19: How patriotic about public education is Senator Kerry where established and successful educational programs exist, such as Head Start?

- ❑ **4) Very Patriotic**
- ❑ **3) Somewhat Patriotic**
- ❑ **2) Neutral**
- ❑ **1) Somewhat Unpatriotic**
- ❑ **0) Very Unpatriotic**

---

[33] George W. Bush, *A Charge To Keep*, p. 91.
[34] *"Head Start,"* John Kerry President, 2004.

Higher Education

> *"To those of you who receive honors, awards, and distinctions. I say 'Well done.' To the "C" student, I say, 'You too can be president of the United States."*
> ~ George W. Bush, Yale Graduation Speech, May 21, 2001

> **"I believe our (higher education) system is basically sound. Our main challenge is to make sure that every American child has the chance to go to college."**
> **~ John Kerry, A Call To Service, p.121.**

The question comes up often. It's on every job application: What school did you attend and what college degree did you earn? When you're getting acquainted with someone, they will ask, "Where'd you go to school?" Both President Bush and Senator Kerry graduated from college and earned additional academic degrees. Having a college education can open the doors of opportunity in America.

Higher education has been a part of the American education experience from the beginning. This country has always held to a faith in the power of schooling. People of faith and patriotism provided the first established "academies." Their religious convictions motivated the founding of our first schools of higher education. Patriots, like Jefferson and Madison, helped found public universities. Many other religious denominations founded Colleges and Universities throughout the 19th century. Over 500 privately supported schools of higher education existed by 1870.

Federal and state government have always seen the value of higher education institutions in serving the public good. Land-grant colleges and universities, especially for the education of physicians, engineers, teachers, agronomists, and other specialized professions, provided for well-trained professionals. Many of these schools became centers of scientific and scholarly research that helped move America to the forefront of education and economic success.

Higher education grew in importance over time. At the beginning of the 20th century, fewer than 1,000 colleges enrolled only about 2% of nation's college age students. Four years ago, over 3,500 colleges enrolled roughly 60% of college age students. Our modern industrial and technological society also offers advanced education through over 6,500 vocational and technological institutes scattered throughout the country.

Our federal and state governments remain committed to expanding access to a college education. It is a patriotic priority. Ask any GI who attended college on the Montgomery GI Bill (Servicemen's Readjustment Act of 1944). Without the federal financial support, these returning service veterans could not have afforded higher education.

In 1965, Congress authorized the Higher Education Act (HEA) to provide loans and grants to a new generation of students. By 2002, over half of full-time undergraduates attending four year colleges and universities now rely upon federal loans or grants. Over the past two decades, the cost of a public four-year college education has increased by over 20%. College and university tuition and fees have risen 38% in just the past decade.

Responding to this growing need for financial assistance, Congress has added numerous financial programs for higher education throughout the years. The list is long: Pell Grants, Perkins Loans, Work-Study programs, Stafford and PLUS Loans. There are also tax credits and tax deductions for higher education. Some legislators predict that spending for student financial aid will top $73 billion if the federal FY 2005 budget is approved. Others think this will not be enough to ensure our historic commitment to higher education, and the common good of the nation.[35]

Q: Is Increasing Access To Higher Education A Patriotic Duty?

President Bush's Record:

In his first presidential campaign in 2000, President Bush made a number of higher education funding proposals, including $6 billion to increase Pell Grants to first year college students and high achievers in math and science in high school (a $1000 increase in each individual

Senator Kerry's Record

Senator Kerry strongly favors enhancing the value of the Pell grants. "I think it's time to ensure that all Americans can afford four years of college. I've proposed a College Opportunity Tax Credit that will help make four years of college as universal as a high school education

[35] *Refocusing Higher Education Aid On Those Who Need It*, Heritage Foundation, 2004. http://www.heritage.org/Research/Education/bg1753.cfm

Bush's Record

Pell grant). He proposed a "College Challenge" grant program to invest $1.5 billion in higher education over five years. This federal funding proposal was to cover one-third of state costs to establish a merit scholarship program. The President's proposals also included complete tax exemption to all qualified pre-paid and tuition savings plans and extended coverage to independent prepaid tuition plans. The cost of this program was estimated to be $275 million over five years.

According to the National Education Data Resource Center, in 2004, President Bush froze funding for Pell Grants and cut $100 Million from Perkins Loans.

At present, President Bush's 2004 budget estimates $3.4 billion for the HOPE tax credit (which benefits mostly middle-class and upper-income students and their families).[36] However, current federal economic policy has left states with nearly $90 billion in budget deficits, and have forced cuts to higher education budgets, resulting in higher tuition, increased class sizes, and cuts to counseling, tutoring and remedial coursework. Rising tuition often mean that students have to drop out and others cannot afford to come.[37]

Kerry's Record

is today," Kerry has proclaimed. He has also proposed a Service for College Initiative that will underwrite college costs for students who give two years of service to their country.[38]

Senator Kerry will help states struggling to bridge deficits and meet their higher education obligations with $25 billion included in his "State Tax Relief and Education Fund" proposal. These additional fiscal resources will be conditioned on better and smarter use of federal higher education funding. Kerry is also proposing a new "I Have a Dream" scholarship program that provides an additional $1000 for students to prepare for college. Among Senator Kerry's high school reforms are programs designed to encourage more states to allow 11th and 12th graders to take college courses. He has proposed to ensure Advanced Placement programs are available in all schools, that math, science and writing instruction programs are strengthened, and he hopes to expand early intervention efforts.

Title IX provides opportunities in education for women. John Kerry has pledged to defend Title IX and expand college opportunities for women.[39]

---

[36] Ibid.

[37] "Making College Affordable for All Americans," John Kerry President, 2004. Http://www.johnkerry.com/issues/college/index.html.

[38] John Kerry, *A Call to Service*, New York, NY, Viking, 2003, p.121-122.

[39] "Making College Affordable...", John Kerry President, 2004.

Bush's Record

Q #20: How patriotic is President Bush about access to higher education?

- ❑ 4) Very Patriotic
- ❑ 3) Somewhat Patriotic
- ❑ 2) Neutral
- ❑ 1) Somewhat Unpatriotic
- ❑ 0) Very Unpatriotic

Kerry's Record

Q #20: How patriotic is Senator Kerry about access to higher education?

- ❑ 4) Very Patriotic
- ❑ 3) Somewhat Patriotic
- ❑ 2) Neutral
- ❑ 1) Somewhat Unpatriotic
- ❑ 0) Very Unpatriotic

CHAPTER 5

Family Values

INTRODUCTION

"The sum of the whole matter is this, that our civilization cannot survive materially unless it be redeemed spiritually. It can be saved only by becoming permeated with the spirit of Christ and being made free and happy by the practices which spring out of this spirit. ~ President Woodrow Wilson, Washington, DC, 1917

The nuclear family has been called the building block of American society. "As the family goes, so goes America," has been a common slogan.

The family was the basic unit of society at the founding of our nation. It educated children, cared for the elderly and infirm, transferred occupational skills to the young, and functioned as the economic center of production. All members participated in the family's support. Men built homes, and barns, hunted and fished, broke sod, felled trees, and protected the family. Women cooked, laundered, made clothing, gardened, harvested, and preserved food. Children had work responsibilities before the age of seven. Single adults were required to live within a family, as boarder or servant.

By the middle of the 19th century things had changed. Childrearing became focused on children's development, marriages were made from love (not just economic necessity), and immigrant families brought their unique cultural heritage to America. By the end of the 19th century many Americans feared that the traditional family had changing drastically - and perhaps not for the better. Birth rates declined and divorce rates increased.

Since the 60s, the American family has undergone further changes. There are many reasons for this. Religious institutions are weaker than ever before; fewer citizens report that they attend church, synagogue, mosque or other place of worship on a regular basis. Marriages are failing at an increasingly rapid rate. Social scientists say that half of all marriages result in divorce or separation.

If family values are in decline, the data on marriage suggests that this is taking place outside of religion amid a coarsening of culture. Respect for life, or what is more frequently termed a pro-life perspective, is often cited as essential to the kinds of human relationships that see beyond the acts of individuals and which discern intrinsic values – an aspect of divinity – within each person.

When citizens acknowledge these truths, they begin to strive for a respect for all human relations. This new vision acknowledges a responsibility to the poor, to those in prisons, to the unborn, and to the common good. Without this sense of higher responsibility, the ethical glue holding America together dissolves. What is necessary for a true healing of America is a firm stance on issues of God, religion and righteousness.

America was founded as a place where people could worship freely and without restraint. President George Washington left us with this keen insight about maintaining a vigorous republic:

> *"Let it be simply asked where is the security for property, for reputation, for life, if the sense of religious obligation desert the oaths which are the instruments of investigation in Courts of Justice? And let us with caution indulge the supposition that morality can be maintained without religion. Reason and experience both forbid us to expect that national morality can prevail in exclusion of religious principle."* [1]

As America has become pluralistic – a people of many nationalities and religious beliefs – religion has retreated from public life. As this privatization of religion has taken place, the quality of public discourse has been altered. Nevertheless, the Declaration of Independence and the preamble of the Constitution still obligate us to be concerned for issues of justice, domestic tranquility, the general welfare and blessings of liberty – for ourselves and our posterity. These are rights endowed by our Creator. These translate today into concern for issues surrounding health care, a clean environment, the roots of crime, broad public access to higher education, and a stable social security system. Taking a Christian stance on these issues gives us the values that translate into a healthy family as well as a firm foundation for America into the future.

[1] Farewell Address given by President George Washington in Philadelphia on September 19, 1796,

Caring for Children

"And there's no better place to start in encouraging healthy choices and exercise than our children...the great strength of America is the heart and soul of the American citizen. People who are willing to dedicate time to make somebody else's life better...To teach children that a healthy body and a healthy mind will lead to a strong future."
~ George W. Bush, Lakewest Family YMCA, Dallas, Texas, July 18, 2003

"Each and every child in this country is valuable because they are our future as a society. We cannot afford to lose a single child to ill-health, under-education, abuse, addiction, jail, or gun violence. America's highest goal should be for every child to grow up to be a successful young adult – healthy, educated, free, secure, and a good citizen."
~ John Kerry, www.johnkerry.com/issues/children

According to the Children's Defense Fund, a Washington-based advocacy group, there are 12 million preschoolers-including six million babies and toddlers-who spend all or part of their time cared for by someone other than their parents. This equates to three out of every five preschoolers being in childcare for some part of every week. Millions more school-age children are in after-school activities while their parents are at work, and over seven million children are left home alone on a regular basis.

Contrast these sobering statistics with the image of Jesus walking among the little children, a picture that literally hangs in most Sunday School classrooms. Jesus always seemed to have had time for children in a first century society that perceived children as treasured property. A Christian is always challenged to ask how he or she can translate the image of being a child of God into a palpable reality in our contemporary society.

Childcare is often family's fourth or fifth highest expense after housing, food, taxes and health insurance. Childcare can easily cost between $4,000 and $10,000 a year.[2] Affordable and accessible childcare is a key factor in allowing parents to obtain and keep their jobs. Federal and state governments, employers, and some labor unions, offer some level

[2] Karen Schulman, *The High Cost of Child Care Puts Quality Care Out of Reach for Many Families*, Children Defense Fund, Washington, DC, 2000.

of assistance to childcare providers and parents. These take the form of tax credits, grants to child-care programs, on-site care, provision for childcare as part of a benefits package, and so on. Yet the diversity of assistance services available still falls short of taking care of the childcare conundrum.

Politicians often declare that children are our nation's greatest assets. Yet the United States is the only industrial democracy in the world that provides no universal pre-or post-natal care; has no national standards for childcare; and has no explicit family public policies.[3] Research shows that good quality childcare can be a great benefit to a child's development. The reality is, many working parents spend too much time and energy worrying about whether their childcare arrangements are good enough, whether the facilities are understaffed, or under funded, or competently managed.

Some people in our society expect mothers to be home looking after their own children. For many families, this is no longer possible given changes in lifestyles that have evolved over the past few decades. Employment and childcare are interrelated. In order for mothers to stay employed, affordable childcare is a necessity. Many families in desperate need for childcare assistance are standing in lines to get it. In California, more than 200,000 children are on the waiting list for childcare assistance. In Florida 48,000 families are waiting, and in Texas, over 30,000 families are still waiting.[4] According to Children's Defense Fund, only one in seven children who are eligible for federal childcare assistance actually get the help they need.

Parents need peace of mind while they are working. Compassionate Christians may find the following two arguments in favor of investing in childcare compelling: first, our society has a moral responsibility to provide safe, quality environments for children whose parents are working; and second; investing in childcare makes sound financial sense.

Research shows that children in good quality early care score higher on reading and math tests, are more likely to complete high school and go on to college, and are less likely to repeat a grade or get charged in juvenile court.[5] The lack of quality after-school options leaves children vulnerable to violence, crime, and early sexual activity.

[3] R. Albelda and C. Tilly, *Glass Ceilings and Bottomless Pits: Women's Work, Women's Poverty*, South End Press, Boston, MA, 1997.

[4] National Women's Law Center, *Low-Income Families Need an Increased Investment in the Child Care and Development Block Grant Now!*, Washington, DC, June 2003.

[5] www.childrensdefense.org

Q: Is it patriotic to supply affordable, quality childcare for all who need it?

President Bush's Record

If elected this November, President Bush plans to freeze federal funding for childcare at the 2004 budget levels, which is almost $5 billion.

Bush's own advisors have acknowledged that 200,000 children technically eligible for federal funds will never see assistance by 2009, at which time they may be too old to qualify.[6] The Center for Budget and Policy Priorities estimates that 365,000 children will not be able to access child care assistance funding during this same time period despite their meeting the eligibility requirements. Add to that total the 100,000 who were dropped from childcare assistance in 2003, as well as the 550,000 children currently on child-care waiting lists, and you have one million families who will be facing very difficult decisions about employment and childcare.[7] More than a few may slip into poverty.

Under Bush's child-care proposal, most families received a tax rebate check for $400 per child. However, families with annual incomes between $10,500 and $26,625 never saw checks. A provision of the Bush tax cut program

Senator Kerry's Record

Back in 1996, Kerry co-sponsored a federal children health insurance bill. He stated that the $24 billion measure provided health care for 5 million formerly uninsured children.[8]

Senator Kerry pledges he will provide states and communities with funding to implement the high quality standards found in the military's childcare system. His proposed program will also improve day-care facilities through uniform standards to improve quality, workforce education, training, and compensation to reward high quality providers and improve safety by requiring criminal background checks.

Kerry proposes to increase childcare funding by $11.25 billion over the next five years.[9] The Early Learning Opportunities Act, which Kerry authored and which became law in 2000, provides funding to help families in the early years of a child's development.

Kerry also promises to fully fund the Head Start program so that every 3 and 4-year-old in need can receive the comprehensive cognitive, social/emotional, health

---

[6] Center for Budget and Policy Priorities: www.cbpp.org

[7] Center for Budget and Policy Priorities: www.cbpp.org/2-4bud-fact.htm

[8] John Farrel, "At the Center of Power, Seeking the Summit," *The Boston Globe*, June 21, 2003.

[9] www.johnkerry.com/issues/childcare

Bush's Record

designed to assist as many as 12 million low-income children was cut out of the final legislation.[10]

The Bush administration has also proposed cuts of $400 million in the major federal program supporting after school activities: the 21st Century Community Learning Centers Program. That level of cuts leaves the program with roughly half of the previous program budget.[11]

Kerry's Record

and parent education services needed for success. Kerry cosponsored the original Family and Medical Leave Act, which gave millions of American workers the chance to take time off for the birth of a child or to care for a sick child or family member. Kerry advocates not only protecting Family and Medical Leave, but would expand the program to help more Americans balance the needs between work and family.[12]

[10] www.childrensdefense.org

[11] National Women's Law Center Report, *Slip-Sliding Away: The Erosion of Hard-Won Gains For Women Under the Bush Administration And An Agenda For Moving Forward*, April 2004, p. 20-22.

[12] www.johnkerry.com/issues/women

Bush's Record

Q #21: Has President Bush been a patriot in his efforts to provide affordable, quality childcare?

- ❑ 4) Very Patriotic
- ❑ 3) Somewhat Patriotic
- ❑ 2) Neutral
- ❑ 1) Somewhat Unpatriotic
- ❑ 0) Very Unpatriotic

Kerry's Record

Q #21: Has Senator Kerry been a patriot in his efforts to provide affordable, quality childcare?

- ❑ 4) Very Patriotic
- ❑ 3) Somewhat Patriotic
- ❑ 2) Neutral
- ❑ 1) Somewhat Unpatriotic
- ❑ 0) Very Unpatriotic

Medical Insurance and Health Care

"America is on the leading edge of medicine for the whole world. We've got the best research and development, we've got great docs, we've got fantastic hospitals. The federal government just cannot run the system as well as docs, professionals, administrators and patients can."
- George W. Bush, Vanderbilt University Medical Center, Nashville, Tennessee, May 27, 2004.

"We're going to make health care affordable for our families and our small businesses and hold down the soaring costs of health insurance and prescription drugs. If I'm President, we will end the days when working people have to negotiate away wage increases just to kept their health care."
- Senator John Kerry, AFL-CIO Executive Council meeting, March 10, 2004

The medical industry is like any other business venture in the U.S. Medical and health care is provided on a fee-paying basis. Hospitals, nursing homes, and clinics that cannot balance their books are forced to lower their standards of treatment or are taken over by more profitable companies.

How to pay for health care insurance is a concern that growing numbers of American families now face. Valuing our family's health is patriotic and the Christian thing to do.

At present, the United States is the only industrial democracy that does not have a system of universal health care. How we pay for medical care as a nation, and who can afford it, are hot topics. Even those who do have medical insurance find that insurance companies often decide their treatment options according to preset formulas that may not meet their individual needs and preferences. Although 70% of American citizens have some kind of private medical insurance, these policies are often limited to covering just emergencies and hospitalization.[13]

It is estimated that over 40 million Americans have no health insurance.[14] A recent report by the Robert Wood Johnson Foundation found that nearly 75% of people under the age of 65 went without health insurance for at least part of the year.

[13] J. Campbell, *Health Insurance Coverage 1998*, U.S. Department of Commerce, Economics and Statistics, Washington, DC, 1999.
[14] James Carville, *Had Enough? A Handbook for Fighting Back*, Simon & Schuster, New York, NY, 2003, p. 189.

Private medical insurance is typically linked to a specific job. Often this coverage ceases if the individual is laid off. Access to medical insurance is also correlated with income and education levels. According to the Institute of Medicine of the National Academies, nearly 1/5 of the total population does not have any medical insurance.[15] They are concentrated in small businesses or are working on a part time or temporary basis. The women in this category who do not have medical coverage cost the economy an annual $130 billion in lost wages and other expenses.[16]

Twenty-three percent of the population has some coverage through Medicaid or Medicare, two federal programs that insure low-income Americans. Medicaid recipients are 70% female because this program provides coverage for mothers and children. There are more elderly women than men who rely upon Medicare. Budget cuts in both of these long-standing federal programs over the past decade or so have resulted in a large number of poor people losing their medical coverage in whole or in part.[17]

A fundamental aspect of women's health is reproductive health. This may include pre- and post-natal care, infant health care, access to family planning information and supplies, and regular screening programs, such as pap smears. Only 8% of female participants in group medical plans are fully covered for hospital maternity charges. At least 25% of all women do not seek prenatal care in the first trimester of a pregnancy partly because they lack medical insurance. Women's Wellness programs provide screening services, but many insurance plans do not cover them.

Q: Should the federal Government institute a national health care policy to cover the uninsured?

President Bush's Record

Over the next decade, President Bush proposes spending $88 billion to insure 4 million more Americans (or 10% of the uninsured).[18] Bush's plan focuses on tax credits that individuals can use to purchase private

Senator Kerry's Record

Kerry proposes spending $895 billion to cover 27 million Americans (65% of the uninsured). Kerry's plan would use tax money to expand employer-sponsored coverage and government-sponsored insurance programs,

[15] "Study: Lack of Medical Insurance Costs US; One Fifth of Working-Age Population Without Insurance," foxreno.com/Associated Press, June 17, 2003.
[16] Molly McGinty, "US Health: Candidates Offer Very Different Health Care Plans," WomensEnews.org, May 20, 2004.
[17] National Center for Health Statistics, 2002: www.cdc.gov/nchs/products/pubs/pubd/hestats/healthinusr.htm Table 1.
[18] www.georgebush.com

Bush's Record

insurance and Health Savings Accounts in which income destined for health can be set aside and not taxed.

Bush claims that his emphasis on competition has slowed what has been skyrocketing health care costs for most Americans. Growth in employer- sponsored health care insurance premiums slowed down in 2004 for the first time since 1996, claims the Center for Studying Health System Change.[19] The Bush Administration has proposed new minimum standards to reduce the frequency and scope of malpractice lawsuits filed by consumers against physicians. The President claims the increases in medical liability add $60 to $110 billion in annual medical costs.[20] Another major initiative of the Bush Administration has been to reduce the cost of prescription drugs.

According to the math calculations of the Bush Administration, seniors now paying full retail price will cut their drug costs roughly in half in exchange for a monthly $35 premium. President Bush has also pushed for bringing generic drugs to market sooner than in the past, an initiative the Administration estimates will save U.S. consumers $35 billion over the next decade.[21]

Kerry's Record

Medicaid and SCHIPS (state children's health insurance programs). By bolstering these existing programs, Kerry hopes to cover all uninsured children in households earning up to $55,000. Individual parents earning up to $37,000 would also be covered under the Kerry funding proposals.[22]

Kerry's proposes to make health care more affordable. He has promised to cut costs by providing families and businesses with premium relief, cutting prescription drug costs; eliminating waste, fraud, and abuse in the health care system; improving efficiency and quality of care; and making malpractice insurance more affordable. He will restore funding to offset current cuts in Veterans' health services authorized by the current Bush administration.[23]

Kerry has worked to ensure women receive access to health care, and has focused particularly on breast cancer research and funding. He was an original co-sponsor of the Women's Health Equity Act to make sure women of all ages receive information and access to highest quality health care. He has also worked to require health plans to cover hospital stays for breast cancer treatment.[24]

---

[19] Milt Freudenheim, "Health Insurance Premiums To Increase Less Than Predicted," *New York Times*, May 27, 2004.

[20] Federal Department of Health and Human Services, *Confronting the New Health Care Crisis: Improving Health Care Quality and Lowering Costs By Fixing Our Medical Liability System*, July, 2002: www.hhs.gov

[21] www.georgebush.com /HealthCare/Read.aspx?ID=2777.

[22] www.johnkerry.com/issues

[23] Mike Glover, "John Kerry Vows to be 'Veteran's Veteran'," *Associated Press*, March 17, 2004.

[24] www.johnkerry.com/healthcare

Bush's Record

According to the Office of Management and Budget, President Bush cut 90% of funding for the uninsured, a change from $104 Million in 2004 to $10 Million in 2005.

Kerry's Record

Of the 14 bills addressing the needs of children that he has introduced in his 19-year Senate career, only one measure has become law.[25]

Q #22: Has President Bush been patriotic in his efforts to improve national health care for the uninsured?

- ❑ 4) Very Patriotic
- ❑ 3) Somewhat Patriotic
- ❑ 2) Neutral
- ❑ 1) Somewhat Unpatriotic
- ❑ 0) Very Unpatriotic

Q #22: Has Senator Kerry been patriotic in his efforts to improve national health care for the uninsured?

- ❑ 4) Very Patriotic
- ❑ 3) Somewhat Patriotic
- ❑ 2) Neutral
- ❑ 1) Somewhat Unpatriotic
- ❑ 0) Very Unpatriotic

[25] DBunker Buster: Kerry has a "Thin" Record on Health Care: www.georgebush.com ; (S. 1510, Introduced 7/1/87; S p, Indefinitely Postponed, 12/4/87; S.2186, Introduced 10/1/96; Senate Amendment 297, Submitted 5/21/97.)

Family Violence

"My Administration is fighting domestic violence and strengthening services for victims and their dependents by supporting local and private efforts and securing historic levels of funding for the Violence Against Women programs at the Department of Justice."
~ George W. Bush, October 9th, 2003, http://usgovinfo.about.com/b/a/033278.htm

"As president, I will put American government and our legal system back on the side of women. I will stand up for their security, ensure their safety, support their rights, and guarantee their dignity. This nation can do no less."
~ John Kerry, March 8, 2003 http://www.johnkerry.com/issues/women/

Violence against a spouse affects all societies, in all income levels, and all racial and ethnic groups. Doctors, lawyers, teachers, police officers, ministers, and many other "ordinary" men beat their wives. Some women have been raised to accept this as part of their husband's role as head of the household. Others may feel that it proves their partner loves and cares for them.

Family violence includes: physical acts like beating and child sexual abuse; verbal and psychological abuse like yelling, intimidation, and humiliation; threats of violence to children or pets; forced isolation; and denial of financial support.

Women – as well as men – can be violent. Women may abuse children and other family members, especially elderly people, as well as people who work for them. Research shows that, in general, women hit children more than men do, but they also spend much more time with children.[26] Women may also contribute to the dynamic of a violent relationship. Sometime they may hit their partner first, for example.

Yet, the vast majority of gender violence is violence against women. According to a government report, the chance of being victimized by an intimate partner is significantly greater for a woman (85%) than for a man (15%).[27] Violence between married couples or other intimate partners is illegal in this country, but is seriously underreported. Rape in marriage was made a crime in the United States in 1993, but in 33 states there are still prosecution exemptions in place

[26] Gwyn Kirk and Margo Okazawa-Rey, *Women's Lives: Multicultural Perspectives*, Third Edition, McGraw Hill, New York, NY, 2004, p. 227.
[27] C.M. Rennison, *Intimate Partner Violence and Age of Victim, 1993-99*, Federal Bureau of Justice Statistics, Special Report, U.S. Department of Justice, Washington, DC, 2001.

for husbands.[28] Some married women and men may not think that rape in marriage is possible-that wives should always be available to their husbands. But laws in some states do not agree with this view.

Since the 1970s, many women in the U.S. have broken the silence about violence against women. In the past, more than a few people considered family violence a mental health problem or personal dysfunction on the part of the perpetrator. Others see violence against women and children as a human rights issue. The U.S. Department of Health and Human Services reported that nearly 900,000 American children were abused or neglected during 2002. According to the *New York Times*, it is estimated that 1,400 of them subsequently died.

Laws addressing domestic violence were first passed in the 1970s. So far, the majority of legislation passed has been at the state level. The federal government can play a major role on the issue of family violence, an issue that touches upon core values of common decency and respect for all of God's children.

Democratic President Bill Clinton signed the Violence Against Women Act (VAWA) into law in 1994. This measure authorized $1.6 billion to be spent over six years to address and prevent violence against women. In 2000, VAWA was reauthorized by Clinton with funds for the National Domestic Violence Hotline, battered women's shelters and community initiatives, training for judges and court personnel, improvements in arrest policies, and legal advocacy programs for victims. The re-authorized law added provisions pertaining to women with disabilities and for senior citizen abuse and neglect.

Q: How can the federal government work toward lowering levels of violence against women and children?

President Bush's Record

As Governor of Texas, Bush spoke out against family violence. In a speech in 1999, Bush pointed out that 176 children had been killed in Texas by abusive parents or caretakers in the previous year. "For every one who dies, countless others suffer in anonymity," said then Texas Governor Bush. "This breaks my heart. I urge you

Senator Kerry's Record

As a prosecutor in Boston, Kerry established one of the country's first offices to assist rape victims. He was an original co-sponsor of the Violence Against Women Act, which has provided over $1 billion for battered women's shelters, hotlines, and other crucial resources.[29] This Act also significantly strengthened federal law by including

[28] National Clearinghouse on Marital and Date Rape, 1998: http://members.aol.com/ncmdr/index.html\

[29] www.johnkerry.com/issues

Bush's Record

to increase funding so our child protection agency can hire 380 new caseworkers to rescue children before they become a tragic statistic."[30]

As President, Mr. Bush initiated the Safe and Bright Futures for Children Program. This program authorizes the federal Department of Health and Human Services to give grants to community and faith-based organizations to provide treatment and support to children in order to break the cycle of violence and child abuse. Through the Department of Justice, President Bush also started the Family Justice Centers program. These Centers will provide comprehensive services for victims of domestic violence in single location. Medical care, counseling, law enforcement assistance, faith-based services, social services, employment assistance, and housing assistance will all be available at these new centers. This year, some $20 million in grants is earmarked to establish 12 Family Justice Centers through interagency efforts and partnership with the local communities.[31]

The Bush Administration's proposed federal budget for 2005, however, cuts support for battered women's shelters and a National Domestic Violence Hotline by 26% below

Kerry's Record

several new federal family violence crimes and enhanced penalties for acts of domestic violence. Kerry has pledged to take this commitment to the White House and support those working to help crime victims and put attackers behind bars.

Along with other Massachusetts congressmen, Senator Kerry worked closely with the Justice Department to award the Lowell Massachusetts Police Department a $535,497 grant to keep their Violence Against Women Office open. The office is a successful and innovative effort to foster collaboration among police, prosecutors, and victims advocates to combat domestic violence and child abuse in the city.[32]

Senator Kerry also signed "A New Agenda for the New Decade," a document that sets forth the following goals:

• Cut the rate of out-of-wedlock births in half by 2010;

• Recruit a million mentors for disadvantaged children;

• Promote policies that help parents shield their children from violence and sex in entertainment products.[33]

If elected president, Kerry has also promised he will make preventing instances of abuse and neglect a top priority. Kerry will support programs such as the

[30] 1999 State of the State Address, Austin, Texas, January 27, 1999: www.issues2000org/2004/George_W_Bush_Families_+_Children.htm

[31] White House Fact Sheet: Preventing Domestic Violence, October 8, 2003, http://www.usia.state.gov.

[32] Fight Violent Crime Against Women: www.johnkerry.com/issues

[33] www.johnkerry.com/issues

Bush's Record

authorized levels of funding.[34] The Administration has also failed to include protections for battered women in marriage promotion programs that are part of its welfare reform proposal. Critics feel this policy could pressure poor women to stay in abusive relationships.

Q #23: How patriotic has President Bush been when it comes to deceasing levels of violence against women and children?

- ❑ **4) Very Patriotic**
- ❑ **3) Somewhat Patriotic**
- ❑ **2) Neutral**
- ❑ **1) Somewhat Unpatriotic**
- ❑ **0) Very Unpatriotic**

Kerry's Record

Child Abuse Prevention and Treatment Act, and expand the primary federal child welfare program to include prevention services rather than just placements after the abuse or neglect has occurred. Senator Kerry has proposed to spend $20 million annually in federal, state and local funds to accomplish these goals.[35]

Q #23: How patriotic has Senator Kerry been when it comes to deceasing levels of violence against women and children?

- ❑ **4) Very Patriotic**
- ❑ **3) Somewhat Patriotic**
- ❑ **2) Neutral**
- ❑ **1) Somewhat Unpatriotic**
- ❑ **0) Very Unpatriotic**

[34] The National Women's Law Center, *Slip-Sliding Away: The Erosion of Hard-Won Gains For Women Under the Bush Administration And An Agenda For Moving Forward*, April 2004, p. 8.

[35] www.johnkerry.com/issues/children/child_abuse.html

Respect for Life

"I believe that life is valuable, even when it is unwanted, even when it is physically imperfect. I believe our society has a responsibility to defend the vulnerable and the weak. And I believe our nation should set a goal: that unborn children should be welcomed in life and protected in law. This is the ideal: a generous society that values every life. I know there are many steps on this road. A democracy is ruled by consensus, not by edict. Laws are changed as minds are persuaded."
~ George W. Bush, upon signing of "Parental Notification Law," June 7, 1999

"I don't think it is right to have a criminal justice system that kills innocent people. Over 100 people have been released from death row in America in the last year with DNA evidence and other evidence showing they didn't commit the crime for which they had been committed, some of them in jail for 10 or 15 years for a crime they didn't commit."
~ John Kerry, Meet The Press interview, December 4, 2002

Respect for life has wide connotations for Christians. Respect for Life means thinking about several interconnected issues: fair and just treatment for those unborn; those with unwanted pregnancies; those who break the law; rare animals and plants on the verge of extinction; victims of the physical, psychological, and environmental damage of war and militarism.

"Thou shalt not kill" might be the most familiar tenet of Christianity, as well as other major religions. The world is more complex now (we rationalize) though wars have been waged – often in the name of God – for centuries. Forced miscarriages have been common down through the ages. All of the Ten Commandments are worthy of our respect and complete compliance, yet our human intellect can contemplate so many shades of gray when it comes to our own particular circumstances. "Thou shalt not kill," is too often passed off as an inconvenient artifact, or so it seems to some U.S. citizens. Christian leaders such as Pope John Paul III publicly oppose the voluntary termination of a pregnancy, but he is also opposed to the war in Iraq because of his consistent respect for life and Catholic faith.

There is no doubt that compassion must prevail. The Bible clearly states that it is our duty as good Christians to look after the disenfranchised. "Religion that God or our Father accepts as pure and faultless is this: to look after orphans and widows in their distress and to keep oneself from being polluted by the world." (James 1:27)

Should we support fetal rights, but not the right of every child to nutritious food, health care, clean air, and opportunities for learning and growth? Perhaps our moral, social, and economic responsibilities do not stop at the moment of birth. What then is the consistent position if one supports life wholly and under all circumstances?

Currently political candidates and parties are very divided on these "respect for life" issues. Both major political parties offer ethical challenges to the conscience of many Christian voters. What is the appropriate role for government in a pluralistic society that celebrates individual freedoms? Where does a good Christian draw the line on family values? How Christian of a nation are we if we decrease individual options and freedoms to support life, but still sell more weapons of mass destruction than any other country?

How we handle the termination of pregnancies, the death penalty, loss of endangered species, and other policies affecting life and death, are not easily answered by the words written by our Founding Fathers. We do need to respect their belief in separation of church and state. We each may have access to a higher power, but we are still governed by laws that rule a democratic Republic. There are many interpretations of what "pro-life" really means if one is a Christian. Government clearly has to play a balancing role.

In a democratic and pluralistic society, citizens debate, politicians vote, and courts interpret and uphold. No matter what laws are passed, modified, amended or even thrown out and dismissed, we each are responsible for our own actions before God. The moral compass of this nation reflects Christian values. This nation's charter legitimizes the rule of the majority vote, and recognizes the rights of the minority. Respect for Life ultimately rests with each and every one of us.

Q: Should respect for life shape public policy on issues of terminating pregnancies, capital punishment, endangered species, and war?

President Bush's Record

The individual right to terminate a pregnancy was legalized for women in 1973. Since that date, however, the right to do so has been increasingly scaled back. Longer waiting periods, informed consent requirements, public funding bans, insurance prohibitions and additional clinic

Senator Kerry's Record

Though Senator Kerry is personally against choosing to terminate a pregnancy because of his Catholic faith and belief in God, he believes that women have the right to make the decision themselves. He believes that the Constitution protects a woman's right to choose and

Bush's Record

regulations are all designed to make it more and more difficult for women to exercise their right.

President Bush vowed to make terminating a pregnancy illegal. In April 2004, the President signed the Unborn Victims of Violence Act, a measure that had squeaked through the Senate on a 50-49 vote. This Act gives legal status or "personhood" to a fetus hurt or killed when a pregnant woman is killed or wounded during the course of the committing of a federal crime.[36]

While Governor of Texas, George W. Bush witnessed the highest number of executions of any other state: 152 executions.[37] Almost 40% of U.S. citizens sentenced to die have come from Texas. Stephen Bright, director of the Southern Center for Human Rights, commented that under Bush, Texas had the fastest assembly line to the death chamber in the country.

Bush's record on saving endangered species, as well as other environmental issues impacting the health of communities and the commons, has been widely criticized by environmentalists (see next chapter on the Environment.)

The decision to bomb Afghanistan and Iraq may trouble some Christians opposed to all forms of war. The atrocities committed against Iraqi prisoners violated perhaps not only Christian notions of respect for life, but the Geneva Convention on War. A group of 27 former senior diplomats

Kerry's Record

to make their own decisions on such private matters in consultation with their doctor, their conscience, and their God. For some, this is an unacceptable compromise of a Christian pro-life position. For others, it reveals a Christian that is respecting the law of the land, while being true to his own faith.

Having worked as a prosecutor, Kerry has examined the issue of the death penalty very closely. After all, he has sent many people to a life in prison because of crimes they committed. Because of the past record of conviction mistakes, Kerry opposes the death penalty.

Kerry is a strong supporter of environmental laws, including the Endangered Species Act, though he has vowed to reform the law to encourage greater flexibility in managing creative solutions.

Kerry voted to support President Bush's decision to go to war with Iraq, but has since voiced dismay at the torture authorized by the U.S. and the stated circumstances that led up to the invasion. Kerry feels that federal government officials misled him. As noted in the National Security chapter, Iraq apparently did not have close links to the terrorists responsible for 9/11. Evidence regarding Iraq's weapons of mass destruction now appears to be lacking. Just the same, Kerry did vote for the invasion and currently does not advocate immediate withdrawal given the current

[36] www.news.findlaw.com/hdocs/docs/abortion/unbornbill32504.html

[37] Citizens United For Alternatives to the Death Penalty: www.cuadp.org/bush/html

Bush's Record

and military leaders, many appointed to key positions by Republican Presidents Ronald Reagan and George H.W. Bush, maintain that the President's foreign policy in Iraq may have undermined U.S. national security.[38]

Q #24: Has President Bush been a patriot (and a Christian) in respecting life?

- ❑ 4) Very Patriotic
- ❑ 3) Somewhat Patriotic
- ❑ 2) Neutral
- ❑ 1) Somewhat Unpatriotic
- ❑ 0) Very Unpatriotic

Kerry's Record

instability in the region. Indeed, Kerry has proposed to increase the number of troops in Iraq by 40,000 soldiers.[39]

Q #24: Has Senator Kerry been a patriot (and a Christian) in respecting life?

- ❑ 4) Very Patriotic
- ❑ 3) Somewhat Patriotic
- ❑ 2) Neutral
- ❑ 1) Somewhat Unpatriotic
- ❑ 0) Very Unpatriotic

[38] Peter Selvin, "Bipartisan Group of VIPS Decries Bush's Policies," *The Washington Post*, June 13, 2004.
[39] "Kerry Calls For More Troops in Iraq, Bolstering US Military," bloomberg.com, May 28, 2004.

CHAPTER 6

Environment

INTRODUCTION

Nothing could be more patriotic for a person of faith, than to be a good steward, to nurture, to protect, to help preserve God's creation.

How is one a patriot when it comes to dealing with the immense environmental problems facing the U.S. today? A myriad of challenges face the next President on the environmental front. Cleaning up our skies, waterways and land requires a delicate balancing act between the responsibilities of public and private actors, the present and the future, and the pocketbooks of us all.

Life, liberty and the pursuit of happiness: These patriotic principles do not easily translate into clear guidance on modern day policy positions on complex environmental issues required by the political leaders of our time. Our forefathers were much more interested in exploiting the vast resources of a pristine America than worrying about the dire consequences of industrial growth.

Life is a very, very broad word. It could refer to millions upon millions of species living on planet earth. Some religions, such as many denominations of Buddhism, explicitly advocate not killing any beings, ever. Our forefathers were Christians and their views on life, and on how important human and other beings are in the greater scheme of things, were shaped largely by the Bible.

Liberty is the freedom to do what one wants regardless of stature, race or religion. We are all familiar with the famous patriotic cry of "give me liberty or give me death." Libertarians focus almost exclusively on this aspect of patriotism. They support a very limited view of government, opposing virtually all forms of regulation, including those impacting the environment. That is only one view on patriotism. Liberty for whom, one might ask? For you or for me? How will our current choices affect our children and their children?

Pursuit of happiness can also be interpreted in many different ways. America has always championed the rights of the individual to seek and find happiness in what then seemed to be a cornucopia of wealth and resources that streamed endlessly to the horizon. Many Americans view the environmental movement as representing an obstacle to their pursuit of happiness, whether it be limits placed on their snowmobiles, jet skis or fishing poles. Yet what about the individual whose happiness results from pristine wilderness, a place that

Jesus turned to for inspiration and insight? Surely, there must be room for all of us in the America of the 21st century?

Some contemporary political, as well as religious leaders, have quoted Scriptures to support the view that natural resources put on this planet by God are here to serve human kind. Secretary of the Interior James Watt, who was appointed by Republican Ronald Reagan, informed Congress that he did not worry too much about depleting the world's natural resources, "I do not know how many future generations can count on them before the Lord returns."

The story of creation is actually our call to stewardship of the earth: God expects and calls us to be stewards of His creation. How can anyone not be awed by the power and beauty of nature as God's handiwork? The Psalms sing of it over and over again. Jesus, in his most challenging hour of spiritual decision, entered the harsh desert wilderness, which gave him strength. Yet we today know that nature can be destroyed. Species have gone extinct. Pollution has compromised both the beauty and quality of the earth and our lives. Nothing could be more patriotic for a person of faith, than to be a good steward, to nurture, to protect, to help preserve God's creation.

More than any other country, the U.S. has been guided by Adam Smith's "invisible hand" and the ideal of a free market. Conservatives such as Republican Theodore Roosevelt linked concepts such as "conservation" to the notion of being conservative when it came to managing natural resources. Though America was founded on the idea of "manifest destiny" and a God-given right to exploit all natural resources, subsequent Presidents have - over time - articulated a more sophisticated approach to the environment. For example, Republican President Richard Nixon created the federal Environmental Protection Agency in 1970 in response to the general public's concerns about clean air, clean water and clean land. That same year, Nixon also signed into law the National Environmental Policy Act (NEPA). Over 80 countries copied NEPA's approval process governing new facility developments.

After more than 30 years of government intervention, the quality of the air most Americans breathe is still considered unhealthy and nearly half of our rivers, lakes and streams are unfit to drink, swim or fish. Since public health is essential to life, liberty and the pursuit of happiness – and economic well-being – all Americans have a vested interest in preserving our environment at the least possible cost.

Since public health is essential to life, liberty and the pursuit of happiness – and economic well-being – all Americans have a vested interest in preserving our environment at the least possible cost.

Safe Communities

"Through aggressive enforcement, the President is now ensuring that companies are cleaning up the pollution they caused at more than 70% of Superfund sites."
~ George W. Bush, The Raw Deal: Kerry's False Environmental Attacks, www.georgewbush.com, April 20, 2004

"The American people have a right to government that will be vigilant and uncompromising in protecting them from toxic chemicals."
~ John Kerry, 104th Congress, S 343, Senate vote 306, July 13, 1995.

Our founding forefathers never really thought about "safe" communities. "What to do with toxic waste?" was hardly a question on the minds of people in the late 18th century, particularly in America. With verdant fields and forests as far as the eye could see, America seemed to be an infinite pastoral paradise.

Still being attached to the notion that America could remain forever an agrarian society, President Thomas Jefferson initially fought efforts to establish any major manufacturing plants here in the U.S.[1] Of course, he changed his mind during the War of 1812 when the shortcomings of being dependent upon imports for critical tools needed for common defense became dreadfully clear. Jefferson then saw the need to have domestic supplies of both raw materials and finished products. Nevertheless, he hoped that America could avoid the squalor of industrial Europe. Over time, the U.S. too, would need to address the consequences of industrial growth.

Public health concerns initially focused on work conditions in urban factories. Of course, like the rest of the world, America would eventually have to deal with the residues of the industrial revolution – its impact on air quality – and the population explosion's large footprint on America's land and water.

Most Americans feel like they deserve to live in a neighborhood that is safe from an environmental point-of-view. Safe places to live, work and play are all considered fundamental rights of not only Americans, but people the world

[1] Tom Sine, *Wild Hope: Crisis Facing the Human Community On the Threshold of the 21st Century*, Word Publishing, Dallas, Texas, 1991, p. 41.

over. Safe air and water were once assumptions, which no longer can be taken for granted. Interestingly enough, former Democratic President Franklin D. Roosevelt offered this warning: "The nation that destroys its soil, destroys itself."

The issue of toxics is among the most perplexing environmental challenges facing the next President. While progress has been made over the past three decades, there is still much good work to do.

Q: How patriotic is the assumption that every American deserves to live and work in safe communities?

President Bush's Record

One of first actions of the federal Environmental Protection Agency (EPA) under current President Bush was to propose to delay regulations developed under the Clinton administration to reduce allowable arsenic levels in drinking water. EPA Administrator Christie Whitman argued that the new standard was too costly for water suppliers in light of minimal benefits to public health.[2] But after a public outcry, the Clinton standards were ultimately put into effect by the Bush administration.

During his first year in office, President Bush signed an international treaty phasing out 12 persistent organic pollutants (including PCBs, dioxins and DDT), but the Senate failed to ratify the treaty.[3] In 2002, President Bush signed into law legislation designed to accelerate the

Senator Kerry's Record

Senator Kerry has long championed the public's right to know about toxic chemicals located in communities where people live. Kerry has consistently cast votes to support the Toxics Release Inventory that requires companies to reveal when they release toxic substances into the environment.

Kerry supports the rapid phase-out of mercury, one of the most toxic substances known.[4] Kerry has also co-sponsored legislation to protect children from exposure to lead and to reduce pesticide use in schools. It was also Kerry that co-sponsored the bill signed into law by the current president to promote cleanups of abandoned industrial sites known as "brownfields" and which provides funding to revitalize these areas so that they can be transformed into productive re-uses.[5]

[2] "Tougher Rules for Arsenic," *Milwaukee Journal Sentinel*, October 7, 2001.

[3] John Heilprin, "Bush Administration Decides Against Making It Easier to Eliminate Toxic Chemicals," *Associated Press*, April 11, 2002.

[4] League of Conservation Voters Presidential Questionnaire, August 8, 2003.

[5] 107th Congress, S 350, March 12, 2001.

Bush's Record

cleanup of more than a half million abandoned industrial sites, increasing funding for cleanups and restoration by 130 percent.[6]

President Ronald Reagan signed into law the "Superfund" program in 1980 that was designed to clean up America's worst toxic hotspots. Reauthorized by President George H.W. Bush, the Superfund program was largely funded by fees assessed on polluters. Those funds ran out in 2003. Taxpayers are now making up the difference and by 2005 will be underwriting virtually all of the toxic cleanups under the Superfund program.[7] Compared to the late '90s, the pace of cleanups under the current Bush administration has dropped by 50 percent.

Kerry's Record

Kerry led the charge to reinstate the "polluter pays" provisions of the Superfund law, voting in early 2003 to reinstate the tax on companies to pay for clean-ups of old toxic wastes.[8] Kerry stated that low-income and minority communities bear a disproportionate share of environmental hazards associated with modern society. He has pledged to create Environmental Empowerment Zones that would empower communities to see that environmental justice issues are included in future decisions about where to locate facilities that impose risks on citizens living in these communities.

---

[6] Brownfields Cleanup - Revitalizing Abandoned Sites in Our Cities and Towns, Environment Issue Brief, georgewbush.com.

[7] *Cleanup Slowdown: How Under-Funding the Superfund Program Harms Communities Across America*, US Public Interest Research Group, August 2003.

[8] 108th Congress, S. 173, January 16, 2003; 108th Congress, S. Constitutional Resolution 23, Senate Vote 97, March 23, 2003.

Bush's Record

Q #25: How patriotic is President Bush when is comes to ensuring that Americans are living and working in safe communities?

- ❑ 4) Very Patriotic
- ❑ 3) Somewhat Patriotic
- ❑ 2) Neutral
- ❑ 1) Somewhat Unpatriotic
- ❑ 0) Very Unpatriotic

Kerry's Record

Q #25: How patriotic is Senator Kerry when is comes to ensuring that Americans are living and working in safe communities?

- ❑ 4) Very Patriotic
- ❑ 3) Somewhat Patriotic
- ❑ 2) Neutral
- ❑ 1) Somewhat Unpatriotic
- ❑ 0) Very Unpatriotic

Air Quality

> *"The Clear Skies legislation will continue the great progress we have made against air pollution...Clear Skies legislation would further improve the health of our citizens, promote new technologies that would dramatically decrease emissions, help communities meet environmental standards and help create jobs for American workers."*
> ~ George W. Bush, White House Speech, September 16, 2003

> *"Reversing his campaign pledge to support limits on carbon dioxide from power plants, the President allowed utilities to decide voluntarily whether they wanted to clean up operations - a backward looking policy to which the administration gave the Orwellian name of the Clear Skies Initiative."*
> ~ John Kerry, A Call To Service, Viking, New York, NY, 2003, p. 152.

Perhaps the one aspect of the environment that is the easiest to take for granted is air. We breathe all the time, but almost subconsciously. We only notice air when we have difficulty breathing. When it smells fresh, or when the wind blows on your face on a walk along an ocean beach we delight in it unconcerned.

Like most of today's modern environmental issues, our Founding Fathers gave little advice when it comes to air quality. The quality of America's air back in the late 18th century was so pristine compared to urban Europe, where "acid rain" emerged as an identified concern in the late 19th century. An American culture that nurtured the idea of "manifest destiny" hardly had time to worry about the long-term impacts of economic development on a land so big, fertile and ripe. Yet the home woodstoves, factories, mills, automobiles, power plants and other components of the modern civilization all eventually took their toll on America's air quality, too.

Since the original Clean Air Act was signed into law by Republican President Richard Nixon in 1970, there have been some impressive gains in air quality. Republican President George H. W. Bush signed into law 1990 amendments to the Clean Air Act that strengthened permit requirements (conforming the law to the approach used with water) and gave the EPA greater enforcement authority over violators.

According to the latest figures released by the American Lung Association in April 2004, 55% of Americans (136 million people) live in areas with either unhealthy air or particulate pollution.[9] This latter particulate pollution category is new. It refers to fine particulates that are easily inhaled into the lungs and can increase asthma attacks, heart attacks and strokes, lung cancers and other forms of premature death. According to the study, 28% of Americans (81 million people) live in areas with short-term particulate pollution whereas 23% (66 million) live in regions with year-round particulate pollution problems. In 2001, nearly 40 percent of children in the U.S. lived in counties that exceed an eight-hour standard of exposure to ozone, a pollutant that can severely affect lung tissues.[10]

Q: Is it more patriotic to develop new comprehensive standards on all major air pollution sources?

President Bush's Record

While on the campaign trail in 2000, presidential candidate George W. Bush promised fresh federal policies to reduce sulfur dioxide, nitrogen oxide, mercury and carbon dioxide emissions from fossil fuel power plants.[11] In February 2002, the President unveiled his "Clear Skies" initiative, a market-based plan that addresses the first three pollutants, but which left carbon dioxide – a key ingredient contributing to global warming – unregulated.

Senator Kerry's Record

In 1984, Senator Kerry introduced the National Acid Rain Reduction Act to reduce emissions from coal power plants and light trucks.[12] In 1990, he fought efforts to weaken the Clean Air Act, pushing for more aggressive anti-smog provisions than were finally adopted and signed into law.

Kerry is a vocal opponent of the current Bush Administration's "Clear Skies" initiative, joining other

[9] State of the Air: 2004, American Lung Association, April 29, 2004.

[10] America's Children and the Environment, US Environmental Protection Agency, http://www.epa.gov/envirohealth/children/findings/

[11] Senator Jim Jeffords, "Jeffords: Clean Air is an American Right," *The Hill*, April 9, 2003.

[12] 99th Congress, S. 1983, December 18, 1985.

Bush's Record

Critics contend "Clear Skies" actually allows emissions to be increased at individual power plants, raises sulfur dioxide allowances by 50%, and increases allowable mercury releases by a factor of three when compared to the Clean Air Act.[13]

Coal is America's most abundant and cheapest fuel to generate electricity. It is also the most polluting, creating acid rain and other problems. Most existing coal plants were exempted from provisions of the federal Clean Air Act when it was passed in 1970. The Bush Administration changed a policy called "New Source Review (NSR)" that extends these previous exemptions for new expansions into perpetuity. Nine northeastern states have filed legal challenges against the Bush Administration air quality policies.[14]

Perhaps the largest accomplishment of the Bush Administration on clean air are new rules that could reduce off-road diesel emissions by as much as 95%.[15]

Kerry's Record

critics who calculated that the reforms actually granted power plant owners greater leeway in releasing pollution into the air. He has also opposed the changes to the New Source Review set into place by the Bush Administration, arguing for a study detailing the public health consequences of not controlling emissions from expanding coal-fired power plants.[16]

Senator Kerry is co-sponsor of the Clean Power Act of 2003, a bill that would reverse many of the changes put in place under the Bush Administration's "Clear Skies" initiative.[17] By 2009, all fossil fuel power plants would have to cap their carbon dioxide emissions at 1990 levels. This would represent the first federal standard impacting emissions linked to global climate change. The bill would also require 75% cuts in sulfur dioxide and nitrogen oxides by the same date. Mercury pollution would be reduced 90%.

Kerry does agree with Bush that power plants and factories should be able to trade pollution emission reduction credits with each other.

---

13 David L. Greene, "Old Power Plants, Clean Air Dilemma," *Baltimore Sun*, September 7, 2001; "The Bush Administration's Air Pollution Plan," National Resources Defense Council, June 15, 2003.

14 "Nine States Sue Bush Administration On Emissions," *Reuters* (Health Wire), December 13, 2002.

15 "Reining in Diesel Exhaust," *CBS News*, April 15, 2003.

16 108th Congress, House Joint Resolution 2, Senate vote 12, January 12, 2003.

17 108th Congress, S. 366, February 12, 2003.

Bush's Record

Q #26: How patriotic are President Bush's efforts to improve America's air quality?

❑ 4) Very Patriotic

❑ 3) Somewhat Patriotic

❑ 2) Neutral

❑ 1) Somewhat Unpatriotic

❑ 0) Very Unpatriotic

Kerry's Record

Q #26: How patriotic are Senator Kerry's efforts to improve America's air quality?

❑ 4) Very Patriotic

❑ 3) Somewhat Patriotic

❑ 2) Neutral

❑ 1) Somewhat Unpatriotic

❑ 0) Very Unpatriotic

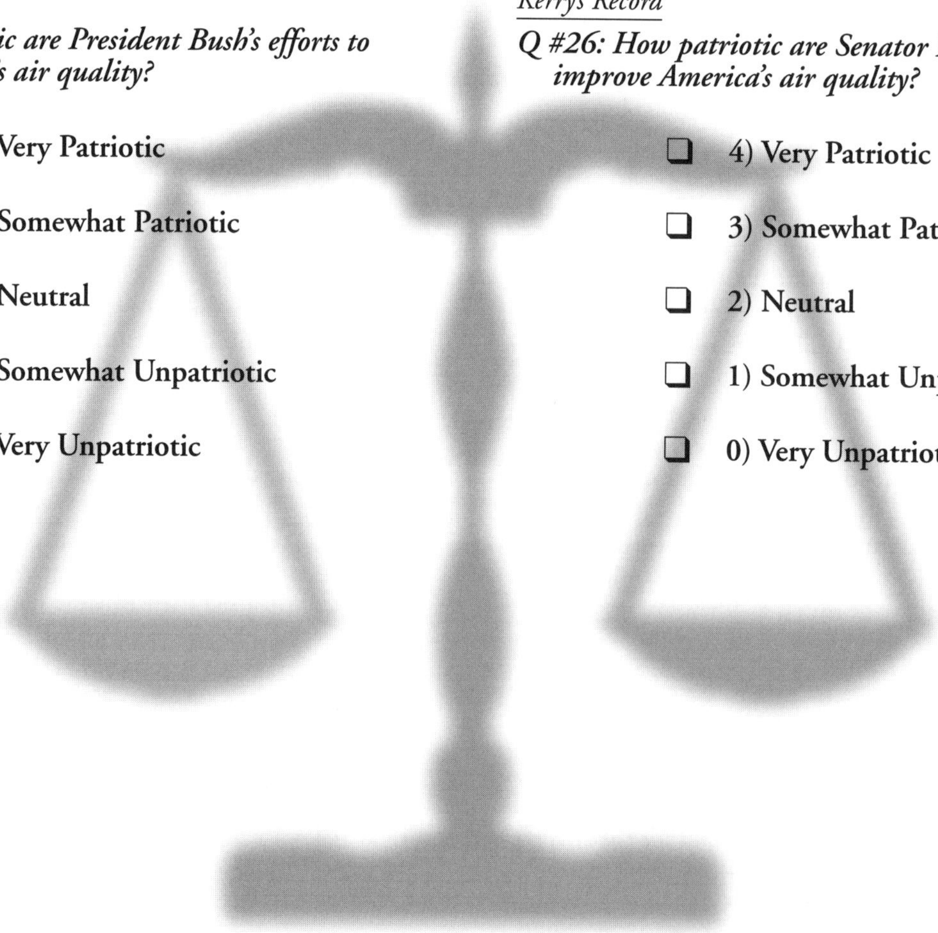

Water Quality

"Today, I want to talk about wetlands. The old policy of wetlands was to limit the loss of wetlands. Today, I'm going to announce a new policy and a new goal for our country. Instead of just limiting our losses, we will expand the wetlands of America."
~ George W. Bush Earth Day speech in Wells, Maine, April 21, 2004

"At a time aggressive action under the Clean Water Act is needed to address our nation's unacceptable water quality, the Bush Administration is proceeding in the opposite direction - softening the bite of the Clean Water Act, and attempting to limit the number of streams and wetlands it protects."
~ John Kerry's Comprehensive Vision for A Cleaner Environment, October 2003, p. 13

Waterways have always been very critical to the economic vitality of America. Rivers, lakes and streams often determined where early populations settled in the New World. Large rivers represented key transportation routes. These water resources also represented fresh drinking water, food supplies and recreation opportunities.

Concerns over the quality of water began to surface most prominently in the 1970s. The Cuyahoga River in Cleveland even caught fire once because levels of pollutants were so severe. Many waterways in urban areas, including Wisconsin's Milwaukee River, were technically "dead" and could no longer support most species of fish. Salmon populations slowly began to decline in the Pacific Northwest, a region in which Native Americans long survived on this traditional source of food and spiritual inspiration.

Water quality was one of a myriad of issues that convinced Congress to pass, and Republican President Richard Nixon to sign, the Federal Water Pollution Control Act of 1972. After being amended in 1977, this law became known as the Clean Water Act. This law gave the Environmental Protection Agency the authority to regulate the types and amounts of pollution that could be discharged into the nation's waterways from a specific point source. It essentially established the framework for funding sewage treatment plants and planning procedures to deal with so-called "non-point" pollution sources (sources that cannot be easily traced and are ubiquitous in many parts of the country).

Saint Francis once wrote: "All praise be yours, my Lord, through Sister Water, so useful, lowly, precious and pure." Water is often symbolic of clean and cool refreshment and cleansing. Yet modern civilization has tarnished this perception. Many rivers, streams and lakes have become little more than large-scale depositories for society's wastes.

Q: What would our forefathers think if they were alive today and knew that nearly half of our lakes, rivers and streams are unfit for drinking, fishing or swimming?

President Bush's Record

In early 2003, the Bush administration launched an initiative that prevents cleaning up the 45 percent of rivers, lakes and streams that remain too polluted for drinking, swimming and fishing. New rules issued by the Bush Administration also now require regional EPA regulators and the Corps of Engineers to seek permission from EPA's central headquarters in Washington, DC before they enforce clean water standards on "isolated" wetlands and seasonal streams.[18]

The Bush Administration has also narrowed the Clean Water Act's jurisdiction to "navigable" waters. According to EPA estimates, this change exempts approximately 60

Senator Kerry's Record

Senator Kerry's foray into advocacy for clean water dates to his first year in the Senate in 1984. He sponsored a bill to provide funding to states to underwrite programs that addressed acid rain's impacts on lakes, a major issue on the East Coast and Upper Midwest.

In the mid-90s, Kerry supported reauthorizing the Safe Drinking Water Act. He supported the following policies:

- New standards preventing unsafe microbe outbreaks
- Requiring most community water systems to report contaminants and public health risks to customers
- Grants/loans for local communities to meet the new water quality standards

[18] Osha Gray Davidson, "Wetlands Left High and Dry in Bush Plan," *Los Angeles Times*, January 10, 2003.

Bush's Record

percent of the country's streams from federal oversight.[19] Twenty million acres of wetlands are now exempt from protection. The traditional acre-for-acre wetlands replacement policy imposed on new developments was substituted with a new policy focusing on restoring the specific functions or ecological benefits of lost wetlands. The "no net loss of wetlands" federal goal is now history.[20]

In April 2004, the Bush Administration announced the largest penalty ever imposed for storm water violations ($3.1 million) at 24 Wal-Mart stores located in nine different states.[21]

Kerry's Record

Kerry opposed the Bush Administration's attempt to delay new limits on arsenic in drinking water.[22] His position on wetlands is to return to the previous status quo goal of "no net loss of wetlands." If elected, Kerry would also restore EPA jurisdiction over "non-navigable" waters, a policy that would reverse the recent changes put in place by the current Bush administration.[23]

Kerry has also supported legislation that would deny additional federal funding for so-called "concentrated animal farming operations" whose runoff discharges contaminate waterways, particularly in the southeast.[24]

[19] Eric Planin, "Administration Establishes New Wetlands Guidelines," *The Washington Post*, January 11, 2003.

[20] Elizabeth Shogren, "Buffers Ebb for Wetlands," *Los Angeles Times*, August 9, 2001.

[21] "US Announces Major Clean Water Act Settlement with Retail Giant Wal-Mart," Environmental Protection Agency press release, May 12, 2004.

[22] 106th Congress, House Resolution 4635, Senate Vote 270, October 12, 2000; 107th Congress, House Resolution 1836, Senate Vote 148, May 22, 2001.

[23] League of Conservation Voters Presidential Questionnaire, August 8, 2003.

[24] 107th Congress, S. 1731, Senate Vote 15, February 6, 2002.

Bush's Record

Q #27: How patriotic is President Bush when it comes to addressing water quality concerns?

- ❑ 4) Very Patriotic
- ❑ 3) Somewhat Patriotic
- ❑ 2) Neutral
- ❑ 1) Somewhat Unpatriotic
- ❑ 0) Very Unpatriotic

Kerry's Record

Q #27: How patriotic is Senator Kerry when it comes to addressing water quality concerns?

- ❑ 4) Very Patriotic
- ❑ 3) Somewhat Patriotic
- ❑ 2) Neutral
- ❑ 1) Somewhat Unpatriotic
- ❑ 0) Very Unpatriotic

Forest Policy

"Almost 750 million acres of forests stand, tall and beautiful across the 50 states. We have a responsibility to be good stewards of our forests. That's a solemn responsibility. And the legislation I sign today carries forward this ethic of stewardship. With the Healthy Forest Restoration Act we will help to prevent catastrophic wildfires, we'll save lives and property, and we'll help protect our forests from sudden and needless destruction."
~ George W. Bush, Washington, DC, December 3, 2003

"I favor a balanced approach to wildfire prevention that provides sufficient resources and responsible fuel reduction around at-risk communities without weakening environmental laws or circumventing public participation."
~ John Kerry, League of Conservation Voters Presidential Questionnaire, August 8, 2003

"I pray you humbly, let them stand, the rugged hills, the broken land. For I do love like any child the creatures of the wild; and every bird that climbs the sky is free to wander just as I, or dwell in peace beside the lake." ~ Saint Kelvin of Glendalough

Forests awaken many of us to the competing demands placed upon America's natural heritage. We draw upon these trees for the building of our homes and other construction projects as well as for inspiration. Managing our nation's shrinking forests is becoming a more complex endeavor over time as policymakers attempt to extract economic value through logging and other timber management practices while still maintaining enough protected wilderness areas to satisfy souls.

Christians note the roots of their faith featured a view of "creation" that valued the protection of the environment. They also note early biblical stories about Abraham, David and Elijah, and Jesus himself all sojourning to the wilderness, whether forest or desert, to hear the voice of God.

Today, many organized religions have passed resolutions advocating the end of all commercial logging on U.S. National Forests, to allow the forests to recover from overcutting and road-building. They include the evangelical

Christian Environmental Council, the National Episcopalian Church, the United Methodists, the Roman Catholic Franciscans, American Baptist Churches, USA, and the Central Conference of American Rabbis. They cite that our National Forests only comprise 3.9% of this nation's total annual wood consumption, which can be offset by conservation. The evangelicals note in their resolution that "The earth is the LORD's, and everything in it." Psalm 24.1

Along with its spiritual connotations, forests and other wilderness areas also happen to provide numerous environmental and economic benefits. Early settlers primarily saw forests as sources of lumber and food. It was Republican Teddy Roosevelt who first saw that conserving forests was but a set of bigger issues facing America: "The time has come to inquire seriously what will happen when our forests are gone, when the coal, the iron, the oil, and the gas are exhausted, when the soils have been still further impoverished and washed into the streams, polluting the rivers, denuding the fields, and obstructing navigation." Expanding upon Roosevelt's point, we know today that the shrinking of the world's forests is just one factor in the extraordinarily and beautifully complex carbon cycles that help maintain life here on this planet earth.

Q: Does respect for God's creation include preserving public forests?

President Bush's Record

One of the first actions President George W. Bush took upon entering the White House in January 2001 was to reverse a Clinton Administration rule that would have banned road building on 58.5 million acres of national forests in 38 states. When a federal judge blocked the rule reversal from taking effect, the Bush Administration tried to reopen public comment on the rule despite 600

Senator Kerry's Record

Senator Kerry agrees with the Clinton Administration's position to ban all new road construction and logging in roadless areas of national forests. He therefore opposes the current administration's "Healthy Forests" Initiative.[25]

Kerry has been steadfast in his opposition to any form of subsidy to encourage logging on national forests and other public lands. In 1999, he voted to strip funding for

[25] League of Conservation Voters Presidential Questionnaire, August 8th, 2003.

Bush's Record

previously held public meeetings.[26] By the end of December 2002, a federal appeals judge reconfirmed Clinton's "Roadless Rule."

President Bush's major policy initiative in this arena is entitled "Healthy Forests" and is based on his claim that 190 million acres of national forests have been mismanaged from a fire prevention perspective. He cited as proof the catastrophic fires of 2003 that scorched more than 6 million acres and killed 20 firefighters. The program allows "fire prevention" activities that include logging for small as well as large, fire resistant trees. It exempts these efforts from the normal environmental review provided by the Nixon Administration's oft-copied National Environmental Policy Act process. Because it also allows the building of new logging roads, environmentalists claim the "Healthy Forests" initiative, could actually increase the risk of catastrophic fires.[27]

Kerry's Record

timber industry subsidies in the Department of Interior appropriations bill and voted in favor of wildlife surveys to shape future forest management plans.[28] Kerry also opposed any government subsidies to build new timber roads. In the year 2000, Kerry cast a vote in favor of converting funds earmarked to make logging on public lands less expensive for corporations in favor of bolstering fire fighting budgets.

If elected Kerry has promised a new "Conservation Covenant" whose purpose is to restore and protect national forests and parks and other public lands for the benefit of future generations. Among the provisions of this proposed program is a more stringent policy placed on private companies who lease forest or other public lands, requiring them to return those properties to their original condition. Royalties paid by private sector companies for resources they have extracted on public lands will be reinvested into protecting the most remote national forests and other

[26] Theo Stein, "Forest Fight Turns Over New Leaf," *Denver Post*, September 4, 2001; Zachaet Coile, "Democrats Urge Bush to Listen to Forest Preservation Advocates," *San Francisco Chronicle*, September 7, 2001.

[27] Sandra Sobieraj, "Bush Proposes Easing Logging Restrictions," *Associated Press*, August 22, 2002; Jim Robbins, "Forest Thinning Challenged As Tactic to Control Fires," *New York Times*, August 27, 2002.

[28] 106th Congress, House Resolution 2466; Senate Vote 266, September 9, 1999; 106th Congress, House Resolution 2466, Senate 272, 14 September 1999.

Bush's Record

Other new forest management practices include giving economic considerations equal weight with ecological ones and doing away with a Reagan Administration policy of giving preference to protecting populations of native wildlife.[29]

Q #28: How patriotic has President Bush been when it comes to managing our national forests?

- ❑ 4) Very Patriotic
- ❑ 3) Somewhat Patriotic
- ❑ 2) Neutral
- ❑ 1) Somewhat Unpatriotic
- ❑ 0) Very Unpatriotic

Kerry's Record

public lands from development pending an economic and environmental cost analysis.[30]

Q #28: How patriotic has Senator Kerry been when it comes to managing our national forests?

- ❑ 4) Very Patriotic
- ❑ 3) Somewhat Patriotic
- ❑ 2) Neutral
- ❑ 1) Somewhat Unpatriotic
- ❑ 0) Very Unpatriotic

[29] Ted Williams, "A Crossroad for Wilderness" *Mother Jones*, September/October 2002; "Bush Administration Proposes Recasting Decades of Forest Policy for the Timber Industry," Defenders of Wildlife, November 27, 2002.

[30] www.JohnKerry.com/issues/energy/index/html, p. 2

Endangered Species

> *"There are a lot fewer salmon in the waters. And the mission has got to be to fight the decline. The mission has got to be to make sure that we understand that without the salmon in the Columbia and Snake Rivers that this would be a huge loss to this part of the world."*
> ~ **George W. Bush, Ice Harbor Lock and Dam, August 22, 2003**

> *"Instead of tearing down the law, I would improve it with a national commission to examine its implementation and ways to enhance it. I would increase funding to protect habitat and work with landowners. I would ensure that federal agencies fully comply with the requirements of the ESA..."*
> ~ **John Kerry, League of Conservation Voters Presidential Questionnaire, August 8, 2003**

How to protect the millions of different creatures found in the U.S. from extinction never crossed the minds of our Founding Fathers. They were too busy thinking about the economic opportunities America's abundance of natural resources represented. Republican President Richard Nixon signed the Endangered Species Act (ESA) into law in 1973. Concern over the bald eagle - an American icon - was among the reasons that prompted lawmakers to legislate a solution to species that were declining rapidly in numbers.

On the 30th anniversary of the ESA, controversy over its effectiveness and cost has reached a new level of scrutiny. Fresh efforts are underway to revise the ESA based on what critics contend are its high cost and low rate of success. Of the 1,300 species of plants and animals placed on the list, only a dozen have recovered and been taken off the list. (Ironically enough, the Bush Administration has just proposed to remove the rarely seen Bald Eagle from the list.) Some highly imperiled species of plants and animals have been on ESA protection waiting lists for decades. The ESA pits a public policy priority to protect the environment against private property rights. Many developers have been frustrated by ESA designations of creatures they perceive as adding little value to society, but whose protection can halt or increase costs of human developments that can offer important services to society.

Some people love mammals and birds, but care less about snails or insects. The ESA puts humans in the uncomfortable position of being God. What is a good patriot to do? In the story of Noah, God commands Noah to bring into the Ark two of every kind of living creature, male and female to keep them alive. The command includes both clean and unclean animals – all are God's creatures). What is more important is that God made an eternal covenant. To Noah and his sons God declared, "I now establish my covenant with you and your descendants after you and with every living creature that was with you. . . . This is the sign of the covenant I am making between me and you and every living creature with you, a covenant for all generations to come: I have set my rainbow in the clouds, and it will be a sign of the covenant between me and the earth." Genesis 9:8-13

Christians have a covenant with God, as stewards of creation. It is both a patriotic and spiritual responsibility to protect species and their habitat. Every rainbow reminds us of it.

Q: Should a faithful Christian support the Endangered Species Act?

President Bush's Record

While the Defense Department's efforts to become exempt from the ESA in 2002 were not successful, President Bush did sign into law military exemptions from 1918 Migratory Bird Treaty Act, which protects 850 different species of birds.[31] The Defense Department has asked for the exemptions in light of urgent preparations for war to combat the terrorist threat.

In 2002, the Bush administration also ordered water to be diverted from the Upper Klamath Lake and Klamath River to struggling farmers in Washington State, a move

Senator Kerry's Record

For more than a decade, Senator Kerry has been chairman or a ranking member of the Senate Oceans and Fisheries subcommittee. One of the key accomplishments in the arena of wildlife protection during his Senate tenure is his authoring of the Marine Mammal Protection Act amendments of 1994. Democratic President Bill Clinton signed this measure into law. Kerry has also authored legislation to ban the use of drift nets that have killed substantial numbers of dolphins and other marine mammals. Kerry was instrumental in securing votes

[31] "DOD Gets Bird Law Altered in Final Authorization Bill," *Environment and Energy Daily*, December 2, 2002.

Bush's Record

that resulted in the largest recorded die-off of salmon in U.S. history.[32]

Due to severe budget cuts, the federal Fish and Wildlife Service (FWS) has not been able to carry out many of its core duties. In May 2003, the Department of Interior announced that FWS had run out of funding to designate critical habitat protection for endangered species. The Bush administration argued that investing in critical habitat was the wrong approach to preserving species because it offered little value to species of plants and animals that were in decline.[33]

The Bush administration in 2003 proposed to de-list gray wolves from the ESA, and re-classify these animals as being "threatened" instead of "endangered." Environmentalists claimed this re-designation was premature.[34] Under the Bush Administration, the FWS also nearly faced a contempt of court citation over its lengthy proceedings to create a protection plan for Florida manatees whose numbers have declined due to collisions with powerboats.[35]

Kerry's Record

for the Sustainable Fisheries Act, which he claims has been instrumental in reviving fisheries throughout U.S. coastlines, including New England's.[36]

Kerry acknowledges imperfections in the ESA. He has urged a cooperative consensus building process to improve it. He opposes granting the Defense Department any exemptions to the ESA. In 1996, Kerry voted against a proposed moratorium on additions to the endangered species list and in 1995, he voted against legislation that would have cut Fish and Wildlife Services funding supporting additional listings under ESA.[37]

---

[32] Paul Rodgers, "Salmon Kill Blamed on Water Sent to Farmers," *San Jose Mercury News*, January 5, 2003.

[33] Guy Gugliotta, "Species Act 'Broken,' Interior Official Says," *Washington Post*, May 29, 2003.

[34] Elizabeth Shoegren, "US Changes Status of Grey Wolf to 'Threatened,'" *Los Angeles Times*, March 19, 2003.

[35] Ludmilla Lelis, "2 Court Rulings Uphold Manatee Speed Zones," *Orlando Sentinel*, March 20, 2003.

[36] John Kerry for President, Environment and Energy Policy, www.johnkerry.com.

[37] 104th Congress, House Resolution 889, Senate Vote 106, March 16, 1995; 104th Congress, Senate Amendment 3479, Senate Vote 30, March 13, 1996.

Bush's Record

Q #29: How patriotic has President Bush been in his efforts to reform the Endangered Species Act?

- ❑ 4) Very Patriotic
- ❑ 3) Somewhat Patriotic
- ❑ 2) Neutral
- ❑ 1) Somewhat Unpatriotic
- ❑ 0) Very Unpatriotic

Kerry's Record

Q #29: How patriotic has Senator Kerry been in his efforts to reform the Endangered Species Act?

- ❑ 4) Very Patriotic
- ❑ 3) Somewhat Patriotic
- ❑ 2) Neutral
- ❑ 1) Somewhat Unpatriotic
- ❑ 0) Very Unpatriotic

CONCLUSION

"Enlighten the people, generally, and tyranny and oppressions of body and mind will vanish likes spirits at the dawn of day." - Thomas Jefferson, letter to Dupont de Nemours, 1816

What do Americans look for when they chose between candidates for President?

Polls show that many voters examine the candidates' records before making a decision. Others select on the basis of party, religion, or perhaps even on a single important issue, such as the economy or national security. A few judge on the basis of appearance or other superficial concerns. Many American voters emphasize that the person they will support for President should be of high moral character. Perhaps no other requirement ranks as high as this in determining which candidate Americans will choose to sit in the Oval Office leading the U.S. and the free world.

Citizens at home and abroad look to the president not just to lead by proposing legislation to the Congress and creating administrative policy, but to lead with moral and ethical example. The president of the U.S. must embrace a panorama of qualities to be an effective chief executive. He must think for the whole nation, so that he unites and does not divide. He must articulate an attainable vision so that he can inspire and not discourage. He must penetrate the issues and uphold the nation's highest values and traditions so that he can speak directly to the concerns of the nation with principled insight, as well as the wisdom of historical hindsight.

In every administration, value conflicts arise. As the country's highest elected official, the President must face the temptations of power and demonstrate respect for the ideals of patriotism, devotion and selflessness. His past actions as well as his present record must inspire and provide an ennobling example that can lift the nation into a renewed sense of patriotism and a vision of infinite possibility.

In preparation for going to the polls this November 2nd, many citizens want to know the candidates as people. The pledges of presidential candidates come and go. Voters want to know a candidate's values even more than his rhetoric. They want to know what's deep at the core of those who are running for president. *The Patriot Test* hopefully has helped you see how each of the chief candidates for the highest office in the land measures up between word and deed. The comparisons made here shed an important light on the fundamental character of each candidate.

Because of the pervasiveness of polls and a sense that the electorate wants a candidate who represents traditional values, every candidate invariably projects an image of God and country. The challenge for the astute voter is to get beyond the superficial and to reach into the heart, soul, and motives of those who aspire to the nation's highest office.

The Patriot Test has been designed to give you insights into the candidates' past and present positions on critical issues, such as the economy, national security, foreign policy, education, family values and the environment. Judgments of character are more difficult to quantify. Our own values often get in the way of seeing people for who they really are. Modern campaign tactics only often blur the lines between candidates in an effort to garner the most votes.

It is now your chance to reflect on how well the candidates' words matched their actions. Have the candidates been open and honest? Have they been credible? Do they demonstrate an ability to unite the country so we can work together to solve our nation's problems?

When these qualities are examined in their aggregate, a reality emerges that can be substantially different from that which the campaign's public relations image projects. The informed voter will not just look at the campaign promises, but the record from time in office. This is what informed voters need to see and this is what helps all of us determine which candidate we will support for president of the United States.

The character of any candidate for the highest office in the land really revolves around **integrity**, the test of words in relation to actions. The 19th century American philosopher Ralph Waldo Emerson gave insightful definition to this challenge when he said, "Your actions speak so loud, I can't hear a word you say." Integrity is walking the talk; it is demonstrating privately and publicly an example of spiritual and moral principles in action. America has historically been strong in moral character and its presidents have more often than not exemplified this quality.

Jesus teaches this same principle. But Jesus also warns the faithful to beware of imposters, of "false prophets" who clothe themselves with the garb and words of sheep, but inwardly are ravening wolves. They may have the rhetoric of sheep, but we need to be discerning. "By their fruits you shall know them" (Matt 7:20).

Campaigns are full of misleading messages and distorted declarations. If the informed voter is going to penetrate beyond campaign public relations and spin to find a reasonably clear picture of the candidate, the record must be compared with the rhetoric. *The Patriot Test* was designed to do just that. This scoring process was developed in the spirit of trying to embrace the type of democracy that our Founding Fathers envisioned centuries ago.

A healthy democracy requires an informed electorate. As President Harry S. Truman said at the beginning of the Korean War in 1950, "Secrecy and a free democratic government don't mix." Voters need a government that is transparent in its motives and actions to make critical decisions.

In order to participate effectively, we need to inform ourselves and insure that our media is independent and free of bias from government or corporations. Currently, information about important campaign issues is limited in its coverage by mainstream media. For example, the major TV networks are condensing their coverage of the Democratic and Republican Conventions to only 3 hours each. Voters need to look to other sources for information on the candidates' position on issues which are important to them.

It may astonish most Americans to learn that the world's oldest democracy is also among the most complacent. According to the International Institute for Democracy and Electoral Assistance, the U.S. ranks 139th in voter turnout if one looks at national elections that have taken place since the end of World War II. During that time period, only 48.3% of eligible voters in the U.S. participated in their democratic rights and duties. Americans lag behind not only countries such as Italy (92.5%) and Germany (80.6%), but Bosnia (82.8%) and Nicaragua (62%). The last time over 60% of Americans voted for the next president of the U.S. was in 1968. Democracy does not take place in a vacuum; it requires the participation of its citizens. It is not only a privilege, but an honor and a duty to cast your ballot.

With these truths in mind, it is not hard to appreciate why John Adams during the Second Continental Congress in Philadelphia emphasized that public virtue is the key to a stable constitutional process. "The only foundation of a free Constitution is pure

Virtue, and if this cannot be inspired into our People in a greater Measure, than they have it now, they may change their Rulers and the forms of Government, but they will not obtain a lasting liberty."

The purpose of this book is to inform you and to inspire you to vote. Beyond voting, there are several other actions one can take in order to be a good patriot. You can share this book with your neighbors. Use it as a discussion tool among your fellow churchgoers, work mates or family members. Don't tell people how to vote, but rather use *The Patriot Test* as an education tool to allow them to make up their own minds. Volunteer in your local community to register voters or to distribute information that will motivate others to vote as well.

The deadline to register to vote is up to 30 days in advance of the November 2nd election. Go to www.fec.gov to print out a copy of the voter registration form. To make sure your vote is counted, we recommend you request an absentee ballot by going to www.fvap.gov/links/statelimks.html. Many electronic voting machines do not yet produce a paper receipt.

Finally, we suggest that you write a letter to your newspaper or church newsletter about the score you gave each candidate as well as about the information you learned from this book. In this way, you will help shape this election

Remember, the future is now. Voting in the election is not only the patriotic thing to do, but the duty of Christians following the examples of this nation's Founders. Let us recognize how the Declaration of Independence, Constitution, and other critical works which shaped our this country of ours were inspired by fresh beliefs in God. Now is the time for America to reinvigorate its democracy.

No matter who is elected this November, the challenges facing America require a return to the patriotic fervor that long ago stirred so many. An optimistic faith in what the future holds is what can still bring us all together. It is time to love our country for what it stood for and for which it still stands. It is time to reclaim our country and remember what the original patriots taught us about a government for and by the people.

ABOUT THE AUTHORS

Peter Asmus is an author, consultant and journalist specializing in political reform, corporate social responsibility and energy and environment issues. His three books include: *In Search of Environmental Excellence: Moving Beyond Blame* (Simon & Schuster, 1990), *Reinventing Electric Utilities: Competition, Citizen Action and Clean Power* (Island Press, 1997), and *Reaping the Wind: How Mechanical Wizards, Visionaries and Profiteers Helped Shape Our Energy Future* (Island Press, 2001).

His articles have appeared in the *Christian Science Monitor, Los Angeles Times, The Sacramento Bee, Orange County Register, San Francisco Chronicle* and many other leading business journals and business magazines. His consulting clients include the University of Southern California, Coors Brewing Company, General Motors, McGraw Hill, General Electric and other Fortune 500 companies.

Fred Krueger is a former Soviet intelligence analyst for the National Security Agency and a campaign manager and fundraiser for the Republican National Committee. An orthodox Christian, Krueger has authored several books on religion, including *A Cloud of Witnesses* (Widf & Stock, 2002), *The Lord's House* (Green Cross,1995) and several other books and publications focused on applying biblical principles to modern-day policy debates.

Warren Linney is a telecommunications executive and former CEO of Cellular One of Western Illinois and Wireless Plus, Inc. He holds a B.A. in Economics from University of California, Davis and a M.A. in Education from Stanford University. He was featured in a Forbes Magazine article about charitable giving.

Published by Patriotic Press, LLC

http://www.patriottest.org

(800) 732-0860

For information on bulk sales please contact us at bulksales@patriottest.org. For information on book tours or educational use go to the website at www.patriottest.org